# "There & ]

**A British Army** ~~~~~~~~

"a trip through my youth spent sailing and flying gliders in Yorkshire; a period working at sea with Shell, and then my 31-year military helicopter flying career including operational deployments to Northern Ireland, the Gulf, Bosnia, Afghanistan and the Central African Republic; and finally, my long journey into the depths of PTSD and eventual recovery from it."

**Lt Col (Retd) Gav Spink - Army Air Corps**

# Foreword

*I was 15 years old. The vivacious young woman I had just strapped into the front seat of the all-aluminium Blanik glider for a trip of a lifetime was dead. Alive one minute and now dead, right in front of me. I had watched them soar upwards on the end of a winch cable at the start of what should have been an exhilarating 20-to-30-minute flight from the Yorkshire Gliding Club overlooking the Kilburn White Horse and then 30 seconds later she was spiraling steeply down from around 150 feet, crashing forcefully into the ground only 100 metres or so away from us. She didn't stand a chance, crushed in the mangled cockpit. My journey into PTSD had begun but would not become apparent for a further 36 years!*

# CONTENTS:

Chapter 1 - Struck out of the Blue.

Chapter 2 - Taking Flight.

Chapter 3 - Fledgling Marine Engineer.

Chapter 4 - Army Officer School – Royal Military Academy Sandhurst.

Chapter 5 - An Infantry Induction to the Real Army

Chapter 6 - Army Pilot's Course 294 – Army Aviation Centre Middle Wallop.

Chapter 7 - First Flying Posting – 3 Regt AAC – Gazelle - Soest, Germany

Chapter 8 - Northern Ireland – Back-to-Back Emergency Tour.

Chapter 9 - Back to Germany.

Chapter 10 - Army Aviation Centre Middle Wallop & the 1st Gulf War.

Chapter 11 - 9 Regiment Army Air Corps – Yorkshire.

Chapter 12 - Gazelle Refresher and Lynx Conversion Course at Middle Wallop.

Chapter 13 - Officer Commanding 661 Sqn AAC Gutersloh, Germany.

Chapter 14 - Bosnia – 2 Tours in One.

Chapter 15 - Air Armaments MoD PE, London then Abbey Wood, Bristol.

Chapter 16 - Second in Command - 1 Regiment AAC in Gutersloh, Germany.

Chapter 17 - Alberta, Canada - Officer Commanding 29 (BATUS) Flight AAC.

Chapter 18 - Management Consultant (!) with McKinsey & Company PLC.

Chapter 19 - Chief Of Staff Army Aviation Centre Middle Wallop.

Chapter 20 - Afghanistan: Commander – UK Aviation Unit - Operation Herrick.

Chapter 21 - On the Ground (and in the Air) in Afghanistan.

Chapter 22 - Counter Insurgency (COIN) Ops - Op HERRICK.

Chapter 23 - Northern Afghanistan based ops – Flying Afghan Air Force Helicopters.

Chapter 24 - Home Again.

Chapter 25 - Head Army Digitisation Training Team Royal Signals HQ, Blandford Forum.

Chapter 26 - Aviation Standards – AAC Centre Middle Wallop.

Chapter 27 - Republique Centrafrican (Central African Republic) Head Current Ops – EURFOR RCA HQ based in Larissa, Greece.

Chapter 28 - SO1 Lessons Learnt – Land Warfare Centre - My last Army posting, and my mental breakdown.

Chapter 29 - Return to Civilian Life.

Chapter 30 - Coming to Terms with PTSD long term.

Copyright © 2023 Gavin Spink

All rights reserved.

ISBN-13: 9798870489155

# Chapter 1.

***S*truck out of the Blue**. It was early January 2009, 36 years after that traumatic but largely forgotten incident that I suffered the first, incredibly frightening, unexplained and completely out of character "out of the blue" doom-laden anxiety attack at my operational base in central Afghanistan. I had been flying helicopters in the Army for 24 years and was nearing the end of a 6-month stint in Afghanistan heading up a specialist air and aviation element of the multi-national campaign to rid the World of the Taliban known as Op HERRICK, I was a fit 48-year-old Lieutenant Colonel, exceptionally experienced as an Army helicopter pilot and tactical commander; veteran of operational campaigns in Northern Ireland, Kuwait, Iraq and Bosnia. I was at the top of my game and doing a job I loved working alongside and embedded within a unit of the best soldiers and Royal Marines the UK armed forces had to offer. I had volunteered for the tour, as I did for all my other operational deployments throughout my career, and felt I was making a significant contribution to the campaign.

I can remember the moment of that first "attack" vividly – I was alone, half-way through a session in the gym, running hard on an indoors treadmill. We often exercised indoors to limit the amount of talcum powder-like dust we ingested whilst exercising – a common problem in the dust bowl conditions in central Afghanistan. Suddenly my heart rate shot up from its normal exercising level of 120 to 130 to over 190 and continued at that elevated level even when I almost fell off the treadmill. My vision tunneled as I fought my way outside into the cooler air, expecting to collapse at any moment and hoping to get within eyesight of someone before I did so. That way *"I'd have a chance of surviving whatever was about to happen"* – that's how weird my thought patterns were. Once I got outside the overruling feeling of imminent doom and likelihood of my impending death disappeared just as quickly as they had arrived, leaving me totally bewildered and wondering what the hell was going on. Neither I, my mates, nor the medics in the base's military hospital knew what had happened to me, my vital signs having all quickly returned to normal; nor were they able to make a diagnosis.

I continued to suffer these occasional "attacks" during the last 4 weeks of my tour, not recognising them for what they undoubtedly were; just aware of how imperative it was "to get outside at all costs into the fresh air of Afghanistan", fresher than that of the HQ complex I often worked in at least, whenever the feelings of "impending doom" struck.

Fast forward a few long weeks I was back home, settling down and enjoying some post tour leave before getting back into the staff job I had left behind some 8 months earlier to train alongside the troops I would be working with in Afghanistan. My family noticed I could occasionally be more distant than I had been after my 6 previous tours away from home on "active duty" operational deployments, but that was it. Eventually I became more used to, still frightened by, but used to, the "attacks" which occurred every now and again with no particular pattern being apparent as to why or when they occurred. Over time, the frequency and effect of the attacks diminished, leaving me with lingering doubts as to my own sanity, but with a prolonged feeling that at some stage I was going to die, well before my time. This was in stark contrast to the rest of my career when I'd never really even thought about the chances of being hurt or killed – I just enjoyed the life, flying Army helicopters at low level, at night on night vision goggles, and across the World in all sorts of weathers, terrains and climates; I also enjoyed leading men and women who had volunteered to fight for their country, at work especially on operational deployments and in high adrenaline sports and adventurous training – I was a good downhill and cross-country skier, very experienced mountain leader, cave leader, sailing instructor and yachtsman, all of which had placed me in situations where death or injury was a distinct possibility and I'd never given the personal risks more than a passing thought. One thing was very clear though, I did not tell anyone in the UK about the attacks, neither the Army medics nor my friends or fellow officers for fear of being labelled as a sicko or somehow unworthy of my rank and position. That was the world we lived and worked in, and to show a weakness could scar me for life, and ruin my remaining career, or so I thought.

# Chapter 2.

**Taking Flight.** I was a lucky child I guess, son of the local Doctor in a small but bustling North Yorkshire town and blessed with regular walking and fishing holidays in the UK with a camping holiday in France thrown in each year for good measure. The oldest of 4 kids, I had a dog to look after and a solid group of local friends, some of whom also later served in the Army and Royal Navy. My father gave us lots of opportunity to develop our characters but always castigated me for not making the most effort academically during my school days. I suppose I was just like lots of other teenage boys, more interested in sports and girls than sweating over exams. As a teenager I was used to mountain walking, dinghy sailing competitively every weekend and whiling away long summer holidays playing aggressive tag with my school mates, gluing together then blowing up airfix models and making small bombs out of bangers around Guy Fawkes night, and shooting rifles at the local range and shotguns on a friend's farm. A little luckier than average but then so were most of the boys I knew, with a great school to go to and above average sports teams to play for. I loved competitive swimming, rugby, and hockey, but hated cricket.

I had loved the outdoors from a very young age. Aged 16, I was used to walking alone across the Lake District in all weathers from youth hostel to youth hostel, was a keen dinghy sailor – a pastime I was introduced to at 8 years old by my father, also a keen sailor, ex RAF Volunteer Reserve pilot, and competitive glider pilot and instructor. My mountain walking and weekends sailing racing dinghies competitively at Thruscross Reservoir on the Blubberhouses moors in Yorkshire hardened me up, climbing mountains in wind and rain and sailing all through the year including in frostbite conditions on the windswept moor taught me to be physically resilient and to be able to work through any discomfort. This held me in great stead later in my military career when I was known as being particularly robust physically, shrugging off cold and wet conditions with ease.

I'd been gliding since the age of 14, working at the Yorkshire Gliding Club at Sutton Bank at weekends and on a local farm to save enough to pay for my next flight. In those days the usual launch method was for a glider to be attached to a long single strand steel cable known as piano wire, with a ring at the end which was clipped into a hook under the belly of the glider that could be released from within the cockpit by pulling the yellow release knob when the glider attained enough altitude or got to the top of the launch. If the pilots didn't release the connection, then the ring and hook automatically disengaged once some back pressure was placed on the mechanism by the weight of the trailing cable. Once released the glider was free to fly around hopefully finding some "lift" or upwardly moving air which would keep the glider aloft for a reasonable period of time. Gliders are always descending so either the pilot found some air which was going up quicker than the glider was descending, or the flight came to an end quite quickly, but usually safely landing into wind on the cliff top grass field used by the gliding club. We learnt how to turn and how to find air going up (known as "lift") in order to soar using thermals.

We also practiced all the emergencies which in a glider are generally pretty simple – don't fly too slowly, and in more modern gliders don't forget to put the wheel down before landing! Wings provide lift to keep the glider aloft because of the phenomenon where air moving over the wing top has to travel more quickly to follow the curved shape, than air going under the wing which goes pretty much straight across. In order for this to happen the pressure above the wing drops relative to the air pressure experienced under the wing, and this differential in air pressure "pushes" or "sucks" the wing upwards[1] – known as "lift".

Flying too slowly in any fixed wing aircraft could result in a stall which is where the airflow over the wing is disturbed enough by the relatively high angle of attack that it breaks away and the lift produced suddenly reduces causing the wing to drop. When turning the lower wing is always flying slightly slower through the air than the outer or upper wing, and so if the glider reaches the stall condition during a turn, the lower or inside wing will stall first which can result in a rapid wing drop, followed by a dramatic nose drop and even inverted flight. If not quickly corrected the wing drop then leads into a "spin" where the glider is spinning rapidly out of control and descending very quickly indeed. The only method of un-stalling the wing and stop the spin and rapid descent is to increase airflow over the wing to gain smooth airflow again. So, the immediate action after a stall whilst turning is to centre the stick laterally, applying maximum rudder in the opposite direction as to the turn and then push the nose down by moving the stick well forwards, something that takes a bit of practice as the natural reaction is to pull back on the stick to try and raise the nose! This incorrect action would simply prolong the spin as the lack of airflow over the tailplane prevents the elevator from working effectively. Height will be lost rapidly before the airspeed builds up enough to break the stalled condition and allow resumption of controlled flight.

---

[1] Lift: An airplane's wing has a special shape called an aerofoil. The aerofoil is shaped so that the air traveling over the top of the wing travels farther and faster than the air traveling below the wing. When air moves faster, the pressure of the air decreases. So the pressure on the top of the wing is less than the pressure on the bottom of the wing. The difference in pressure creates a force on the wing that lifts the wing up into the air.

When flying at Sutton Bank (The Yorkshire Gliding Club) there was a cliff edge which faced into the prevailing westerly wind, so usually the aim was to get a launch attached to the winch cable and be pulled up high enough to fly forwards and reach the upwardly moving air where the wind was forced upwards over the cliff. Once there one could fly in both directions along the cliff hopefully above the cliff face and stay aloft for as long as you wanted to. Occasionally the cable would break during the launch – the single strand piano wire used those days was prone to snap whenever it got bent whilst it was being pulled out by the tractor used to return the hook end to the launch point and so we often practiced for this eventuality. When a cable break occurred the immediate action was to push the stick forwards to lower the nose, which might have been pointing up by about 30 degrees above the horizon at that stage, and to regain or maintain safe flying speed. The reaction of the pilot needed to be instinctive and pretty quick but be moderated if you were still quite low – or the nose could be pushed down too much, and the glider fly straight into the ground. Once in stable descending flight the pilot had to quickly decide whether to land straight ahead, with the drop over the cliff approaching rapidly, or aim the glider for a point a few feet above the cliff edge and fly over the edge, often at very low level – so low that people walking along the cliff edge path would sometimes have to duck! Once over the edge the pilot turned the glider along the cliff face and, now below the ridge, had to soar along the cliff making sure the wings didn't hit it and hoping to get enough lift to climb back up to a safe altitude. If this wasn't possible then the glider would be turned into wind again, away from the cliff, and a farmer's field chosen as a rough landing site. The one thing we had to be very aware of and avoid at all costs after a cable break was flying too slowly – if we did this and then attempted to turn, the lower (and slower) glider wing could enter a stall, dropping suddenly on that side and the glider placed into an attitude (the start of a spin) where it didn't have enough height to recover from.

By 16 years old I was a qualified solo[2] glider pilot, having been given a day off school on my 16th birthday to "go solo" – the youngest age allowed in the UK at the time. I'd also been exposed to death in its' ugliest form, sudden and traumatic, twice in the last 2 years – the first a vehicle accident we came across where we were unable to help the already dead driver, the second time I watched the accident unfold, and then tried to help, as the extremely attractive, full of life young woman, who I had just strapped into the front seat of a Blanik glider for her first ever flight was crushed almost to death by the impact when the glider spun into the ground some 100 metres in front of me. Sadly, the glider had for some reason been flown too slowly immediately after a cable break and it entered an incipient spin from which there wasn't enough height available to allow the pilot to recover safe flight. She died whilst we were trying to help her breathe, holding her head straight to try and allow oxygen to reach her lungs. Even though my father was a doctor he never discussed this incident with me, and I bottled up any feelings I had afterwards, never discussing the event again until 2015. One incident I remember very clearly was flying a circuit at the Yorkshire Gliding Club in my Ka6. I looked down below me as I turned towards the airfield boundary at about 300' above the ground ready to open the airbrakes and descend to land, when with a massive roar three US Air Force F105 Thunderchief fighter-bombers known as "Thuds" passed underneath me and raced across the airfield at very low level. Luckily the turbulence they caused didn't quite turn me upside down – I'm sure they never even saw me!

---

[2] Solo: qualified to fly alone – a significant step for any aviator.

I had a busy year in 1976 and 1977, gliding most weekends, and during the school holidays driving the winch or the tractor and painting all the club's buildings to earn enough cash to continue flying whenever I could. I spent 3 two-week periods at sea on a Bermuda rigged 3 masted 140-foot sailing schooner called the "Malcolm Miller". This was run by a charity, the "Sail Training Association" as one of 2 very near identical yachts with square sails on the foremast, multiple sails on and between the fore and main masts and a mizzen sail hung from the aft mast. This rig made for very exciting sailing and needed the crew (us) to run up and down the rigging like pirates on the Black Pearl, setting and doffing sails day and night. The aim was to give young people, some very

Figure 1 - The Malcolm Miller.

disadvantaged, experience of sailing a big yacht at sea, living and working in teams (watches) in cramped conditions often in very rough weather. The first trip was a gift from a friend's father, the second 2 I earned by putting 100% effort into that trip and being asked back to oversee 13 first- timers manning one of 3 watches – the yacht ran a standard 3 watch 24/7 working rota. My first experience of leading others, I absolutely loved it – the stronger the wind and rougher the sea, the more it ticked all my "adventure" boxes, sailing from the south coast to France via the smaller Channel islands, over to Gothenburg from Harwich via Amsterdam and all along the south coast of England from St Ives to Chichester, all fantastic experiences, especially the north sea crossing at night in a force 8 gale! Back to gliding, I gained my Bronze "C" qualification and then my "Silver "C" which meant I had proven my ability to stay aloft alone for over 5 hours, use thermals to climb over at least 1000m above my launch release height and flown cross-country for over 50km before landing in a field. The 5-hour flight was particularly memorable as I could hardly walk afterwards, my legs and bum being completely numb from sitting very upright in the club's Polish made Pirat glider for such a long time! I completed my "Silver[3]" distance flight in a club owned Schleicher Ka8, a very slow and gentle glider which nevertheless was very good at going up in the slightest updraught. I was very lucky and did most of my solo flying in a Schleicher Ka6CR which my father had bought a half share in, this being a lovely aircraft to fly, comfortable and reasonably high performance for its day.

I was unlucky enough to be caught up in my own gliding

---

[3] Gliding awards were known as "badges" and started at Bronze, working up to Diamond level of achievement.

accident on 19th March 1977, when the Falke motor glider[4] I was P2 in (not the pilot in charge) hit a small tree on take-off, spun through 90 degrees and crashed one wing first into the ground a short distance from the cliff edge at the Sutton Bank White Horse.

*Figure 2 - YGC - my Falke accident (faint "X" marks the spot)*

However, we were lucky, the glider was severely damaged but we both climbed out unaided. Had we not hit the tree we almost certainly would have arrived at the White Horse cliff edge without

---

[4] Motor glider: an aircraft which is classified as a glider but has a motor which can be used to facilitate a self-launch or to maintain height if there is a lack of thermal or other lift available (used to prevent having to land in a field in some modern motor gliders)

enough airspeed to fly properly and I probably wouldn't be here to tell the tale. Literally! I was almost thrown into a powered aeroplane with an instructor within 30 minutes of the crash and flew around for approximately an hour before landing safely. Sadly, the Falke pilot killed himself in another accident a few years later. No one ever discussed the accident with me, but I always considered that "that was MY accident" and that I would always be okay flying in the future. Although not discussing the accident probably resulted in me bottling up any fear or concerns for years, the thought that *"that was my accident"* always enabled me to remain very calm when dealing with emergencies in the air in later life – some potentially very dangerous; as attested to by my passengers after a very tricky situation flying my Lynx helicopter in Bosnia in 1996 – but that is jumping the gun somewhat and will be covered later. Looking back, it wasn't really surprising that I was to suffer from PTSD later in life.

I passed my driving test on my first go 3 weeks after my 17th birthday and was lucky enough to be allowed to borrow the family car very occasionally to take girls out to dinner or the cinema in nearby York.

I was very lucky to be taught how to drive properly after passing my test, by David Chaplin[5], a bluff Yorkshire police driving instructor in my father's ex-police Ford Consul GT; this was a trade against my father teaching him to fly. Under David's tuition I learnt to read the road, measure risk effectively and learnt when it was okay to drive really fast, and when driving at the posted limit was way too fast for the conditions. I do remember one incident

---

[5] Unfortunately, David died in a flying accident many years later whilst I was away on an operational tour, so I never got a chance to pay my respects.

which of course happened when I had sneakily taken the car without express permission – a cat ran out just in front of me and I skidded to a halt (no ABS in those days) literally missing it by a whisker! I got out and checked the hedges and ditch but no sign of the cat – so that was a relief. As I drove off the car went bump-bump-bump in time with the wheels. I stopped again but no cat. I thought I must have worn a flat patch on the tyre which skidded the most and realised there was no way my father wouldn't know I'd had the car out without permission. Luckily however, it must have just been the tyre getting very heated in one spot because the noise had gone by the time I got home. To this day, apart from a near death experience on, or nearly off the back roads of Wales and a totally unavoidable major accident in Germany in 1995 I have never had a car accident – David obviously taught me well.

Three of the boys in my class at school had birthdays in the same week and we celebrated our 18th together in a local village hall hired for the night, dancing and rocking to Slade, Led Zeppelin and the Sweet, getting drunk on a heady mix of John Smiths bitter and woodpecker cider – it was an excellent end to childhood.

# Chapter 3.

**Fledgling Marine Engineer.** My father found it hard (in his defence he was an only child) to cope with me questioning his authority from around 16 or 17 onwards, and I decided to forgo my confirmed university place at Leeds University reading civil engineering and work for Shell as an apprentice marine engineer to get away from any control he had over the direction my life was taking. That might sound selfish, but I needed to be in control of my own destiny, not live a university life funded by him; and Shell offered a salary and a training program over 2 years based in a technical college specialising in marine engineering.

On joining Shell, I went to Riversdale Technical College situated in one of the roughest areas of Liverpool and studied for an OND in mechanical engineering over the next 2 years and learnt all about girls. The Toxteth riots of 1981 were literally a stones-throw away from the college and where I lived during my first year; the atmosphere when I was there in 1978 and 1979 was toxic to say the least. My first real girlfriend was a nurse at Alder Hay Children's Hospital, and we had a lot of fun in her nursing accommodation and in my shared student house over the 2 years. I learnt to rock climb, eventually happily leading Hard Very Severe rated climbs in Wales and the Lake District during weekends off. I also nearly killed myself and 2 climbing friends whilst driving too fast back to Liverpool one night in my souped-up Honda civic when I "lost it" on a greasy mountain road corner. Somehow, I managed not to hit the rock bank on my left and not career over the cliff edge on my right. I learnt to manage risk and fear during climbing and from that near accident – I always drove fast but never stupidly so after that incident.

My time with Shell was both interesting and fun. After I got the surprisingly excellent results of my 2 years studying for an OND in Marine Engineering at Riversdale Technical College I spent 5 months on a ship in the surprisingly rough North Sea, working as a junior engineer, and was then offered a place on BSc degree course studying marine engineering at Southampton, all the while being handsomely paid by Shell. I jumped at the chance and packed up my life in the MG Midget which had replaced the Civic, and with tonneau cover on, I headed south.

Over the next 4 years I spent 6 months in Southampton studying, then a 2-week holiday, a 5-month stint working on ships around the World with Shell as a marine engineer, then another 2-week holiday. During the stints on ships, I deployed to the North Sea on the MV Northia, flew out to the Far East 3 times and nearly deployed to the 1982 Falkland's war.

*Figure 3 - MV Northia (author centre)*

**18**

The MV Northia was the biggest tanker I sailed on at 130,000 tons, approximately 288m long. On her I helped look after giant diesel engines with each piston about one meter across, learnt to machine parts for the engines from big blocks of steel called blanks when we didn't have the required spare part, and got used to working the maritime watch system, supposedly 4 hours on, 8 hours off, but more usually 6 on and 6 off with all the extra duties we each held.

During 2 of the 3 Far East trips the ships had no air-conditioning and so we had to leave as many doors open as possible to let the draft through our cabins. The engine rooms were fed by enormous electric fans, and these were mounted at the top of the engine-room next to the funnel. Part of my job as junior engineering officer was to walk around all the engine-room spaces twice every "watch" checking on the machinery – you could tell if it was about to go wrong because it would be running hotter than it usually was or would be vibrating when it was normally smooth running. The aim was to spot something going wrong before it failed and change the bit over whenever we had a quiet period. Checking the cooling fans at night was scary – they and the engine-room were so noisy that we wore ear defenders all the time we were on duty. Opening the fan room doors we would then step inside and close the door behind us to do the checks, but the problem was that some massive insects, looking almost like blue bottles, but the size of a sparrow, loved hiding in there during the evening, and so we would get the fright of our lives opening the door to find ourselves surrounded by these critters all trying to get out! We did some very unusual things whilst at sea, and I packed as much as I could into enjoying life, sailing a lot, continuing to rock climb and walk in the mountains whenever I could.

In Borneo we used to anchor up just offshore occasionally and take a lifeboat ashore.  Shell ran an amazing "officer's club" where we could relax, swim, use the beach and eat lobsters, tiger prawns and other shellfish until we could eat no more - all for pennies, washed down with plenty of Victoria Bitter.  Being on 2 venerable Shell tankers which were sold for scrap during my trips at sea on them was an amazing experience – around 10 miles offshore, we set the engine controls to full speed ahead, then ran up the 8 stories of ladders up through the engine-room to pop out onto the deck just below the bridge just in time to watch as the Chittagong shoreline in Bangladesh got larger and larger as we steamed towards it at 15 knots.  A 35,000-ton tanker weighs quite a lot, even when empty, and the momentum carried us up the beach between 2 other decrepit skeletons of old tankers to the ships' final resting place, with the bows almost overhanging the road along the beachhead.  Immediately, what seemed like hundreds of Bangladeshi locals swarmed up ropes and over the rail then hauled up their cutting gear behind them.  Their task was to cut the ship into small parts which could be dragged off and sold as scrap.  Whilst they were doing that, they lived in what must have seemed like luxury – our old cabins, but without running water or changes of bedding!  Within 10 minutes of beaching the small crew of ships officers climbed down the ships boarding ladder for the last time, jumped in a minibus, and headed off to Dhaka, the capital, for an internal flight to India then onwards to home.  Unfortunately, the incoming Fokker propellor plane crashed right in front of us, and we had to spend a night in a local hotel eating "chicken and chips" rustled up from somewhere dingy.  The "chicken" on my end of the table had a very long tail – so I'll leave you to surmise exactly what we were eating!

*Figure 4 - SS Achatina.*

The second time I helped take a tanker onto the beach at Chittagong (one was the SS Acavus[6] and the other its sister ship, the SS Achatina, but I can't remember which was first) we had no problems, and the crew got home as planned.

On one of those trips prior to scrapping the ship we sailed from Singapore to Darwin in Australia via the Arabian Gulf, and when we got there the main steam driven turbine seized whilst we were a mile or so off the loading area. This was our only engine and we needed it to be able to slow down, the momentum of a big tanker

---

[6] All Shell (UK) tankers were named after shells found in the sea. MV stands for Motor Vessel, SS for Steam Ship!

being enormous. We didn't have enough room to turn around and so we rammed the loading jetties at about 5 knots. Apparently, we caused over £1M in damage to the loading area, a considerable sum in those days!

Finally, my last trip at sea (although I didn't know it then) was to fly out to Singapore again, and after a wait of a few weeks I flew on to Japan to pick up a brand-new type of tanker. Unlike my previous ships where we worked in 3 watches manning the engine room 24 hours a day (4 hours on in the engine room, 2 hours working on ships systems such as electrics then 6 hours off, repeat…) this ship had a fully automated engine-room. That meant we could work a single 8-hour day shift and then take turns to be on standby for the night in case the engine room monitoring computers noticed a problem. If they did the standby engineers (always 2 on a shift) had 60 seconds to acknowledge the "alarm" by pressing a button beside their bed and in various locations all over the ship's accommodation block, and another 3 minutes to get down into the engine-room control-room to cancel the alarm. If either of these time gates wasn't complied with the major alarm sounded and all the engineers had to get down into the engine-room. Obviously, we didn't want that to happen. I arrived in Singapore by Virgin 747, having spent most of the long flight chatting up the stewardesses in the crew area at the tail of the airplane to be told the ship (the MV Eburna) wasn't ready yet and we had to stay in Singapore for 3 weeks until it was. I had a swanky hotel room in the Merlin Hotel (5*) and we were offered either full board, or BnB with $50 a day to spend how we liked (including paying for food). As you could buy a small dish in the local market for $1, and 3 dishes made a veritable feast, there was no decision to be made. Hotel meals cost a lot more, but I rarely did this, preferring to explore and eat street food whenever I was hungry. We did occasionally take a taxi to Jurong Pier where the crew of 18 shared dishes of amazing oriental and Thai food for a small proportion of the $50, washed down with copious quantities of Tiger Beer, or cans of Victoria Bitter which I had a liking for after my 2 previous trips to the far east[7]. I also visited the Raffles Club Bar for a few Gin Slings during my stay there. Three weeks grew into 5 and during the day I would sight-see and took up windsurfing which was largely unknown in the UK at that time. My dinghy sailing knowledge came in very handy, and we blagged our way into Changi Beach Water sports club, built on the site of the infamous WW2 prison camp, to start my windsurfing career. Having rigged a sail (not difficult for a dinghy sailor) I then stood on the board and drifted out into Jurong Bay where hundreds of tankers were moored up waiting to be loaded with their cargo. I could not work out how to turn properly, due to there being almost no wind, until I was about a mile off the beach and hit the side of a big tanker and fell off. Climbing back on very quickly (as I had seen sharks swimming around beneath me during the trip out) I used the ships' side to turn the board around and pushed off towards the distant Changi Beach. The wind then came up a bit helping me to work it all out and eventually I got back to the shore unscathed. I enjoyed this new sport so much that I bought a long board windsurfer out in Singapore and shipped it back to Europe with me. Eventually I became an expert windsurfer and instructed many soldiers in the sport through my earlier days in the Army. After 5 weeks in Singapore, we flew up to Aichi Dockyards near Nagoya in Japan

---

[7] Interestingly, the Dutch Royal Family had a tradition for all seafarers working for Shell Tankers (UK) Ltd (which is part of Royal Dutch Shell) and Queen Beatrix paid for and provided 2 beers a week to both officers and sailors. In the Far East the beer of choice was "tinnies" of Victoria Bitter originally made in Melbourne Australia.

and took over our new ship from the staff at the shipyard.

Sailing the MV Eburna over to China and up the Yangtze River to Shanghai was the absolute highlight of my time with Shell. No British ship had sailed as far up the river since the infamous "Yangtze Incident[8]" in 1949 and our arrival was feted by the Shanghai Mayor who came aboard for drinks with the captain before we were allowed to head off into the "city" by government taxi. Now a place of millions of people, in the early 80's it was the size of a small town, and the highest building was around 5 stories, scaffolding was made from bamboo and not steel, and everyone used bicycles to get around – there were very few unofficial cars.

We were only allowed to shop in the Shanghai Peoples Friendship Store, an amazing labyrinth of government controlled small stores under one roof. I bought some jade, some silk and a couple of silk pictures for my walls back home – you know the ones: with misty mountains and a dragon or 2 flying around in the distance!

---

[8] In April 1949, with civil war raging in China between the Chinese Communist People's Liberation Army and Nationalist Kuomintang forces, the frigate (a type of warship) HMS Amethyst was ordered up the Yangtze River to act as a guardship for the British Embassy in Nanjing. When it was around 70 miles away from Nanjing, Amethyst came under fire from Communist artillery batteries on the northern bank of the river and while attempting to evade the shelling it ran aground. During the incident 17 members of the crew were killed and 10 wounded, including the captain, Lieutenant Commander Bernard Skinner, who later died.

*Figure 5 - Shanghai via MV Eburna.*

From Shanghai we sailed back to Singapore then on to India, and into the Suez Canal looking for someone to buy our cargo of some 30 thousand tonnes of unleaded petrol. The Suez Canal zone was still littered with the detritus of the 1956 Arab Israeli Suez Crisis (or war!) and it was interesting to see what seemed like hundreds of tanks destroyed in their shell scrapes on the Egyptian side. In the Bitter Lakes we had to stop to allow the one-way-at-a-time northern part of the canal to empty and our "convoy" of commercial ships to continue its journey up to Port Said (the entrance to the Mediterranean). During our wait we were subjected to hawking street vendors arriving by dhow shouting up at us and trying to sell everything from hashish to Egyptian relics to their sister! Eventually having exited the Canal we sailed up through the Mediterranean to Cyprus (where we took the lifeboats ashore for a picnic and decent swim) and then Gibraltar and across the Atlantic to the US Eastern seaboard, where we anchored off Miami for a while, and then finally we sailed South to Caracas in Venezuela where we unloaded.

*Figure 6 - Rough Seas, MV Eburna, Indian Ocean.*

Having cleaned the tanks we then headed for Europe, but part way across the Atlantic were told the ship (the "MV Eburna") had been chartered by the UK MoD in a process known as STUFT (Ships Taken Up From Trade) as it was required to take a cargo of fresh drinking water onboard at Ascension Island and to then steam South to the rapidly building crisis which became the Falklands war. Unfortunately for me Shell insisted I had to get off and fly home from Ascension as I had my final 6-month stint at Southampton finishing up my degree to do. I sadly left the ship and watched all the news bulletins over the next few months hoping that it didn't get sunk. I did see it again in the middle of San Carlos Water in one news clip where it was storing and deploying water to the many troops ashore during a major air to ship attack by the Argentinians – the one where the Argentine Pucara[9] ground attack aircraft were trying to sink a few ships and a British army Gazelle helicopter was sadly shot down by one of our own ground-to-air missiles. I had no idea at the time that I would eventually end up flying some of those very same missions in Germany and the Gulf and later train younger pilots to do the very same in readiness for Gulf War 2, but that was some time in the future of course!

At the time I was ready to go back to sea with Shell, but I felt I needed some time in a job ashore to allow me to find a girl and settle down a little. I asked Shell if I could do that for a couple of years, but they said not yet. A friend who had been on the MV Eburna with me was leaving Shell as he had just got married and was interested in joining the Army, so I said I would go with him to the 1994 "ARMEX" Army Exhibition in Harrogate for a couple of days to see what it was all about.

The Army was in full recruiting mode having done brilliantly in the Falklands, and I loved it! Gary decided it wasn't for him, but I managed to get a place at the Army Officer Selection Board at

---

[9] The FMA IA 58 Pucará (Pucara means Fortress) is an Argentine ground-attack and counter-insurgency (COIN) aircraft manufactured by the Fábrica Militar de Aviones. It is a low-wing twin-turboprop all-metal monoplane with retractable landing gear, capable of operating from unprepared strips when operationally required. The type saw action during the Falklands War and the Sri Lankan Civil War.

Westbury[10] at short notice and having passed that test and an interview at their Bordon HQ the REME (Royal Electrical & Mechanical Engineers) offered me a place at Sandhurst starting in January 1985 - in about 4 months' time, and I was set. I gave in my notice and told Shell I was leaving to be an engineer in the Army. Shell was brilliant about it and said my place was open to come back if I decided I didn't like the Army.

I decided to set off around the Southern USA hitch-hiking for a few (nearly 5) weeks for some fun before I got to Sandhurst. I had a brilliant time meeting lots of really nice people who were falling over themselves to help me when I explained why I was carrying a Union jack on my big ruscac. Apart from my first night in New Orleans, where I arrived in perfect time to go and see Bruce Springsteen on his "Born in the USA" tour, I was nearly always offered a bed for the night by the last lift of the day. I did spend a night in the police/sheriff's cells in Georgia where I fell afoul of a law that you had to be carrying a minimum number of US dollars in cash to avoid being classified as a vagrant. The rather overzealous policeman in his Dodge Charger locked me up after arresting me for hitch-hiking, which was also illegal, doing a full-on tire-smoking U turn (a la Dukes of Hazard!) across the interstate median to stop me at gun point in the process! He did relent later and gave me a cell with an open door for the night and provided a full breakfast the next morning courtesy of the local diner – who says American policemen are all bad dudes?

I eventually flew home from the States in time to go on an

---

[10] AOSB as it is now called puts applicants through a 2-day selection course, testing mental agility, physical fitness, team spirit and leadership ability on a high-pressure selection course.

attachment with the REME unit attached to 2nd Royal Tank Regiment (RTR) who were based in Fallingbostel in Germany. I spent nearly 6 weeks with them learning all about soldiers, their undying humour, and their life in the Army. I helped the unit's REME Captain recover a Sherman tank which had been found buried in a bog since WW2 and which would become the Regiment's gate guardian. That was a fun task, wading up to our chests in freezing mud to attach steel hawsers to the tank's chassis then pulling it out using a Foden armoured recovery vehicle. I also took part in Cambrai[11] day celebrations – for some reason the Army usually celebrates big failures, but this was a celebration of the first major tactical win using tanks; painting an RMP car yellow, throwing "thunderflash" flash-bangs around the mess accommodation etcetera (known as "high spirits"). One of the thunderflash landed between the twin windows, a bit like secondary double glazing, blowing glass all over the room and scaring the occupant considerably – but that was his fault for being in bed and not joining in the fun. However, apart from that short, one week task I found the life of a REME officer to be pretty boring and spent most of my time with some of the RTR subalterns who were having the time of their lives leading troops of Chieftain tanks in training and exercising across the exercise areas and fields of Germany, preparing for the Russians to invade. At the end of my time with 2RTR, the Commanding Officer asked me if I'd like to join them instead of the REME, and I left Fallingbostel on a real high, wondering whether the REME was the right place for me after all.

---

[11] Cambrai day is celebrated by the Royal Tank Regiment – it marks the first real success of British tanks in the offensive battle, close to the village of Cambrai in Northern France on 20th November 1917

After spending Xmas day with my parents and younger brother & sisters back in Yorkshire I headed off to Val d'Isere for a week's skiing with a couple of friends before reporting to the Royal Military Academy Sandhurst at 11:00 on Monday 7th January 1985 to start the next phase of my life.

# Chapter 4.

# Army Officer School – Royal Military Academy Sandhurst.

I arrived at the Royal Military Academy Sandhurst (RMAS or simply "Sandhurst" as it is known) in Camberley on an icy cold Monday morning – 7th January 1985 with a very short haircut and driving my newish VW Sirocco Storm, one of the few cadet officers to own a car. Within an hour I had an even shorter haircut and had slipped and fallen many times as we tried to march back and forth all over the ice-covered parade ground and over the "wish-stream"[12] carrying my old life in a battered suitcase, and my new life (uniform and PT kit) stuffed in a mark 58 pack and associated webbing, with a Self-Loading Rifle (SLR) slung over my shoulder. Sadly, the car was locked away for the next 5 weeks and keys stored by WO2 Callahan Scots Guards, Amiens Company's Sergeant Major!

I was assigned to 15 Platoon under Colour Sergeant John Bradshaw of the Queens Lancashire Regiment and Captain Colin Tadier of the Royal Horse Artillery. They would be guides and mentors for myself and the 30 or so other young officers in the platoon through the whole of our Officer training at Sandhurst. From inspecting my room to throwing live grenades or running 8 miles with full battle kit, they would be alongside us all the way. The first 5 weeks were definitely the worst. As a fit 25-year-old with significant man management experience already under my belt I felt the constant oversight and pressure to conform very deeply and wondered whether I'd made the right choice leaving Shell.

---

[12] Those who have served as a British Army officer will always remember the "wish stream" a concrete banked stream running through the middle of the Academy grounds and the place of many dunkings during our time training to be an Officer.

Colour Sergeant Bradshaw could see my turmoil and when I asked him if the field Army was really like this, he took me aside and gave me a strong bit of advice – stick with it. He told me that it wasn't at all like this in the Field Army and would, after the breaking-in process was over, become much more focussed on building skills and teamwork – both of which I looked forward to. So, I stayed with it. After 5 weeks of beasting we passed "*off the parade*", a rite of passage where we had to show we had learnt to march, project our voices, dress smartly without a speck of dust on our uniform etcetera, things got easier and more interesting. Bayonet practice and live firing with the General-Purpose Machine Gun (GPMG), Self-Loading Rifle (SLR) and Colt 45 pistol followed alongside section and platoon level tactical training - living and operating in the field in all weathers.

During the 5-week breaking-in process Exercise First Flush on 23rd, 24th and 25th January 1985 was our introduction to living in the field. We deployed on foot onto "Barossa" the hilly sand and heather covered RMAS training area, built bashers[13] and cooked field rations, sleeping for some of the night in the minus 23°C frost and snow for 2 nights whilst starting to learn to conduct patrols and ambushes. The importance of looking after one's kit became clear and keeping dry whenever possible also became second nature. The importance of good boots also jumped into our consciousness, as many of the Company suffered from cold injuries due to wearing boots with steel grips – which allowed to cold to penetrate the wet leather in the near freezing conditions prevalent during our first few months training. As we approached the Easter break, the first time we would get more than 2 days off since arriving at Sandhurst, I

---

[13] A sleeping shelter using anything available – branches and leaves, a poncho, anything to keep the rain off.

had a long chat with Captain Tadier about my chosen "Arm" - the Royal Electrical & Mechanical Engineers. I really didn't want to continue down that path and was looking for something to transfer to in order to be more of a front-line soldier – the CO of 2RTR had assessed my character well during my time with them. Luckily for me Captain Richard Folkes of the Army Air Corps (AAC) was also a directing staff officer in another Sandhurst training Company, and he had somehow learnt that I had already qualified as a pilot. He and Captain Tadier arranged for me to attend Army pilot selection at AAC Middle Wallop – this was a whole series of exercises designed to show if you had good hand/eye coordination and in those days consisted of weird manual tests to show you could balance a table tennis ball on a moving plate, tell which way up an aircraft was from looking at a picture of the instrument panel of an aircraft in various under control and out of control flight situations, and cope with being spun around on a moving chair before doing something demanding good dexterity; and having passed that with apparently a very high score, I was selected to attend AAC Grading Flight in my Summer holiday.

Flying Grading was a 3-week course where the aim was for ex-military instructors to assess your initial flying skills and more importantly assess how quickly you could likely improve, taking on new skills, should you go forwards to the Army Pilot Course to train as a helicopter pilot. The flying was on the venerable De-Haviland Chipmunk and my instructor was retired Wing Commander "WingCo" Hawkins and I did well, my gliding experience being very similar to power flying except the Chipmunk had an engine!

*Figure 7 - My Flying Grading Course (2nd from left front).*

The 3 week period covered everything from starting up the engine (which used 2 shotgun cartridges to power the turning mechanism until the engine "caught" and ran on its own), through taxiing to and from the runway (a difficult manoeuvre due to the chipmunk being a "tail dragger" with a big nose which blocked the view forwards until the aircraft was just about to take off) to taking off and climbing away at set parameters (heading, power setting, flaps setting, and height to level off at were all taught very precisely just as if we were on a parade ground) and then how to adjust the attitude of the aircraft in flight with more or less power and the accompanying trim positions so that the aircraft would fly hands-off whenever required. We learnt to turn, climb, and descend which were all very easy for me after my gliding experience and then were tested a little on navigation and map reading. Due to my previous flying experience, I was allowed to spend a couple of the "spare" sorties learning to barrel-roll and loop the aircraft – what fun! Obviously, as I'm telling this tale, I passed.

*Figure 8 - Unit Cave Leader - author right.*

Heading back to Sandhurst, even without a holiday, my mood was incredibly buoyant – as long as I didn't fail the AAC pilots' course, I would be flying helicopters for my career once officer training was finished. The remainder of my ground-based officer training passed in a blur. I had also been offered a full commission by the AAC which meant I could serve for as long as I wanted to assuming I got promoted to major – the REME had only offered a Short Service Commission (3 to 6 years).

During my time at RMAS others dropped by the wayside for many reasons, they were all determined young men who had volunteered to serve their Country and we felt sorry for them failing the long selection & training process, but we learnt that only the

*Figure 9 - Author with GPMG.*

best was good enough as we progressed. Memorable incidents included being asked to give the next-door officer cadet, a serving cavalry General's son, a lesson in clothes ironing, knocking on his door only to find him trying to press creases into his trousers whilst wearing them! He didn't pass out of Sandhurst. Another was spending 3 days on the run in Germany – being hunted by regular soldiers and the German civilian police force alike. We were tasked to escape and evade to a point some 100 kilometers away, and I found it was great fun. We were dropped in various locations across Western Germany and tasked to find our way to our RV having been stripped naked and issued just a rudimentary photocopy of a map, an NBC[14] suit and allowed our own boots but without laces, and a water bottle. Walking through fields in the dead of night our group of 4 would find ourselves surrounded by cattle or constantly electrocuted as we walked into electric fences unseen in the darkness, both making us jump, one with an involuntary "urrgghh". We swam a river and crept through a railway tunnel, expecting to be told "hands-up" at any time. Occasionally we would hear the dogs searching for us. A German farmer gave us some meat pies one night – that was pretty much all the food we ate for 3 days. Having reached the final RV without being caught we were then subjected to resistance to interrogation training (RtoI) for a period which seemed like days but was probably only 12 to 18 hours or so. Very realistic and some found it incredibly stressful. Keeping to the "fab four" was all that was required – name, rank, army number & date of birth. I would have to undergo a more in-depth form of RtoI training later on as pilots were believed to be more prone to capture than most serving personnel and due to our job, we would have considerable amounts of very useful information in our heads whenever flying near any enemy. At one point in this 3-week-long final exercise, we were living in "harbours" – safe hidden areas where a platoon or section of men/women could get a bit of sleep-in turn, plan and move out again to accomplish tasks and missions. We were visited regularly by the directing staff who came to the harbour every couple of days, bring details of a dead-drop where we could pick up more rations

---

[14] NBC: Nuclear Biological & Chemical. NBC protection consisted of 2 layers of gloves, over-boots, a respirator and a suit. The thick multi-layer rough surfaced suits were impregnated with charcoal and were to be used in case of attack by Soviet Forces. The complete ensemble was designed to allow you to "fight" for around 6 hours before needing to be replaced. It was so hot and claustrophobic that most servicemen and women were rendered pretty much useless after just a few hours marching, digging trenches or flying.

and also details or "orders" for our "missions" for the next few days. We realised that the directing staff had no communications with us (there were no mobile phones in 1985) and we decided to move our harbour a short distance without telling them being particularly fastidious in hiding our trail and camouflaging all "sign" as we moved. That gave us a whole day to rest and catch up on sleep until they found us. We persuaded the directing staff that they must have misheard our map grid reference (our exact location on a map), and even though they knew we were telling porkies, they let us get away with it! The final exercise was a great success, and afterwards we travelled in coaches back to England knowing that it was highly unlikely that we wouldn't be passing off the parade ground and marching up the steps of "Old College" behind the College Adjutant on his horse very shortly.

Other highlights of my time at Sandhurst were going orienteering which I loved and continued competing at through all 31 years I spent in the Army; and walking onto sports parade in a wetsuit carrying my windsurfer on the first occasion we were allowed to choose our own sport - we had a sports afternoon on Wednesday and Friday to promote team ethos and enjoyment of the outdoors, and this always started with forming up in platoons on the parade square. CSM Callahan saw me dressed in black neoprene carrying my board and came tearing across the parade square bellowing at the top of his rather loud voice "what the hell did I think I was doing?", however when close up he grinned widely and said I could continue as long as I agreed to teach other officer cadets how to windsurf, which of course I did. I also managed to squeeze in a Joint Services Cave Leader Course which being a climber I passed with flying colours and meant I could take soldiers caving once I finished at Sandhurst.

*Figure 10 - Half of 15 Platoon (author front left, Capt Tadier RHA front right).*

At the very end of my officer training, in August 1985, one of our platoon (my best mate Paul), died in a car crash the night before we were both due to pass out of Sandhurst as young officers. There was no time to mourn and certainly no time to discuss how sad his waste of life was, we enjoyed our last night as a rite of passage and then everyone in the platoon split up to go to our various Regiments or onto further career specific training the very next morning.

One incident on that second to last night at Sandhurst still stands out in my mind some 37 years later. I and 3 of the other young about-to-become commissioned officers decided to go and visit the ladies' officer's accommodation at about 23:00 hours, after we had all drunk rather a lot at our pre-leaving RMAS Dinner Night. We

40

had crept around the academy and climbed a drainpipe and some vegetation to reach a balcony in their accommodation and spent an hour or so there chatting and drinking more (illicit) booze. Having decided we had better get back to our lines as we had a very early start for our commissioning parade day we climbed back down and were nearly back at Amiens Company lines when we were spotted by one of the full Colonels based at Sandhurst. We were ordered to stop, which after initially pretending we hadn't heard him we did and gave our names before being told to get to bed. The four of us wondered what would happen in the morning. Well, we soon found out. When the whole Company (around 80 young officers to be) were lined up on New College square at 05:30 the Company Officer Commanding – Major Tom L of the Royal Anglian Regiment, appeared in front of us at 06:00. He ordered the 4 of us to march forward and then started to berate all of us about our ungentlemanly behaviour. The 4 of us looked at each other thinking we about to be "back-termed" and made to spend another 6 months at Sandhurst when we heard Major L say "… and only 4 of you have kept up to the best traditions of the British Army Officer and the rest of you should take note..." Oh wow, we weren't going to be back-termed at all. Later whilst I was part way through my first 4 months flying in Northern Ireland a newly arrived Commanding Officer needed to be flown around Belfast – that CO was a newly promoted Lieutenant Colonel Tom L and fate had it that I was to be his pilot during his initial tour of his "patch" in Belfast. The look on his face when I turned in my pilot's seat and lifted my dark visor just before we lifted out of Girdwood barracks was priceless.

Immediately after leaving Sandhurst, I spent a few weeks at Middle Wallop going through initial AAC officer induction then was posted to Paderborn in Germany for 6 months from December 1985 until April 1986, attached to the infantry as an infantry platoon commander to further develop my leadership skills and gain an understanding of infantry battalion tactics which should help me as an AAC pilot later in my career.

# Chapter 5.

**An Infantry Induction to the Real Army.** I was based in Paderborn as a platoon commander with 1st Bn Queens Lancashire Regiment – a significant test for a Yorkshireman, but one which I really enjoyed and which confirmed to me that I had done very much the right thing in leaving a safe job with Shell to join the Army and, hopefully, fight for my Country.

It was made doubly difficult by the fact that the previous AAC officer attached to them had been a Walter Mitty character who wore weird uniform decorated with bits of braid that shouldn't be worn by AAC officers, and also wore a set of Army "wings" – the badge of a qualified helicopter pilot. He had told them he was already qualified as a helicopter pilot and also that he had earned a mention in dispatches during the Falklands campaign. Both were found to be complete lies, and he was later sacked from the AAC and the Army in due course. So, I had to prove myself as an honest and trustworthy character on top of being from the wrong side of the Country!

I learnt to live and operate from trenches in freezing weather – often minus 10°C or so in Germany during the winter, and fight under arduous conditions, spending around 5 months deployed into the wintry countryside of Germany in charge of 30 well trained and quietly aggressive British soldiers – salts of this earth. My time spent getting on with it whilst slowly freezing in my sailing dinghy as a youth helped enormously. Charging around the German countryside in an armoured personnel carrier was fun, even the very first time out on exercise when the Commanding Officer Lt Col David Black OBE told me, with a grin, to lead the Battalion move out of barracks to the exercise area. It was a test of my navigation and map-reading skill but I got them all there on time.

We occasionally got to see the "enemy" during these exercises – usually a battlegroup from another Brigade, and on one occasion I was leading a Company sized attack on foot through some "enemy" trench positions when I bumped straight into Lt Dan Nicholas, a friend and brother Army Air Corps officer on his attachment to the Royal Scots infantry, and we stopped to have a chat. Our respective soldiers were running past us open mouthed yelling "*kill him Sir, f\*\*\*ing kill him*"!

During quieter moments between exercises, I found the time to organise a couple of caving weekends and then participated in a big Army expedition descending the Berger Cave in the Alps near Grenoble. This was a 3-day descent underground and return to the surface using single rope techniques to cover long drops and then the more normal crawling and squeezing through dark and wet passages seeing some spectacular stalagmites and stalactites on route, with underground waterfalls and long winding river sections – fantastic! Whilst we were deep underground the Alps were subjected to a very strong hailstorm and we emerged from the dark depths to find cars and tents trashed. Luckily for me my motorbike was unscathed as I had parked it close under a big solid tree. Just after returning to Paderborn, I left the Battalion to start my flying training; my platoon, and the company they were part of deployed to Northern Ireland.

# Chapter 6.

## Army Pilot's Course 294 – Army Aviation Centre Middle Wallop.

Back in the UK in January 1986, I now started on Army Pilots Course 294 at Middle Wallop – the home of the AAC. The first part of the year-long course was spent flying the Chipmunk again (we had flown it for our 3-week grading course halfway through my time at Sandhurst, remember?) learning how to fly accurate circuits on take-off and approach to landing, navigate by day and by night, using the air to ground radio and generally having a lot of fun. The instructors were all retired RAF officers. I was allocated to WingCo Hawkins again, and their job was to train us to Power Pilots Licence (PPL) standard so that we could operate an aircraft safely in a civilian aviation environment. We did no tactical flying during this phase. On nearly every single flight we would be given at least 2 emergencies to deal with – one of which would always be a practice engine failure but in different phases of flight every time. So, we might have the power chopped just after take-off, whilst flying around at height or whilst making a recce or approach to land in a field site, some situations trickier than others! The aim during these drills was to get the aircraft down on the ground without crashing no matter where or when the "emergency" occurred. We would always round out just above the field surface and put power on again to climb away from the ground just before touching down as actually landing in a rough field might well damage the aircraft – or us!

Everything we did in the aircraft was demonstrated first, usually once, by the instructor and then we had to replicate it every following flight whenever that technique was needed. It was a fast and hard learning curve, but fantastic fun. Each aspect of every flight was graded, once you had been shown how to do it properly you were expected to automatically do it that way every time. Each flight, more and more elements were added to our repertoire – it was intense and just to make it easier (not!) there was a process called "going on review"; if your performance wasn't up to scratch on 2 consecutive occasions in a row then we were placed "*on review*". First you had an instructor change and were given a few more flights to iron out the problem. Then, at the end of the review period, you had to fly a test flight with senior management – and they would either pass or fail you, on the spot. To fail meant being forced to leave the AAC, and going to another Regiment, Arm or leaving the Army altogether – harsh perhaps, but it meant only the best got through and expensive training time wasn't wasted, the Army couldn't afford to lose helicopters or men through bad flying, it was dangerous enough anyway with losses through technical failure and inclement weather being all too common, as I would later find out.

*Figure 11 - 1st solo on Chipmunk "Echo".*

My gliding experience proved extremely useful and the first

time I was told "you have control" followed by a practice engine failure I put the aircraft perfectly in position to round out just above a suitable field, having "side-slipped" steeply into it. My instructor couldn't believe it!

There were a couple of interesting moments during our Chipmunk phase. I went solo very quickly because of my gliding experience, so was ahead of the drag curve for a while. My instructor liked doing aerobatics, so he once again taught me how to loop, barrel role and stall turn. Another pilot of the course also had a PPL, so he too was taught a few aerobatics as well. Two of the other pilots in my cohort managed to touch wings whilst illegally trying to do close formation flying during a daylight navigation sortie, putting a small dent in each wing, one on top, the other underneath – I believe that cost them both a few crates of champagne to the civilian engineers who looked after the Chipmunks for us, and I'm certain the instructors never found out! Myself and the other PPL holder individually decided to "mess around" one night sortie – we were supposed to be doing a small navigational trip around Salisbury, out to Bath and back – but that seemed a bit boring, so I decided to liven it up with some night aerobatics with my lights off so no-one would notice (there were lots of Middle Wallop aircraft out night flying every night the weather was appropriate in those days). I had a great time rolling and looping over open countryside just to the south of Salisbury away from the route being followed by everyone else and was recounting the details in the bar later when the other PPL pilot turned completely white. It turned out he had been doing the exact same thing at the same time in the same location. Only luck had prevented us crashing air to air into each other!

Having passed the Chipmunk phase without a serious hiccough, we then moved on to the Gazelle helicopter for the first part of our military flying training. This time our initial instructors were civilians, usually retired military instructors, for what was called Basic Rotary Training, and they were then replaced with some of the best military pilots in the AAC during the Advanced Rotary Flying phase – these were normally senior ranks or SNCOs (soldiers of Sergeant or higher rank) because their career profile was normally to fly continuously once qualified until they retired from the Army, so they built up flying hours and experience quickly once qualified. Unlike soldiers, officers were usually expected to fly for a couple of 2 – 3-year tours, then do staff jobs usually behind a desk for a while, and if lucky come back to flying as a Squadron Commander in charge of 12 helicopters and 90 -120 men and women for a 2 to 3 year tour. After that they would usually do another staff job or 2 and if very lucky fly again, albeit occasionally, as a Commanding Officer of a Regiment (usually consisting of 3 flying squadrons and a headquarters squadron with a REME workshop in tow). The advanced rotary phase SNCO instructor pilots or Qualified Helicopter Instructors (QHIs) were here to teach us how to fly the Gazelle helicopter as a reconnaissance vehicle, finding and reporting on enemy movements and positions and bringing artillery fire to bear, and if lucky after further training control air to ground strikes against these enemy targets by fast jets. That meant flying ultra-low level tactical sorties, sometimes at speed, sometimes creeping around in the hover – all of which had to match the tactical scenario at the time.

We also had to learn to fly in very poor weather, and in the clouds so that we could reposition from one airfield to another using a radar guided approach to descend out of the clouds, or if forced up into cloud by rising ground or subject to descending cloud during a tactical sortie we could survive long enough to get back safely onto the ground having flown in the clouds for a while.

The first basic rotary phase sortie in the Gazelle was a "freebie" – i.e. we were not marked on anything during the sortie, but simply given a chance to enjoy flying it (it proved to handle similarly to the chipmunk but obviously capable of flying much lower, slower and also faster) and hovering, a whole new skillset which didn't come naturally. My basic rotary instructor was Mr Perrott, a very calm and friendly individual who oozed flying experience from every pore. He was able to allow us to get within nanoseconds of crashing and then take control at the very last moment without seemingly thinking about it. This ensured we learnt the most from every situation where we got it a little bit wrong and put the Gazelle "out of shape".

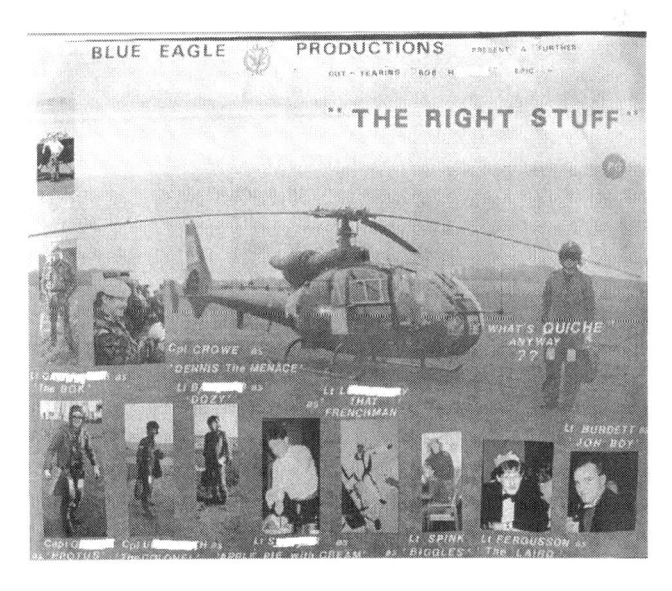

*Figure 12 - Army pilot's Course 294 (1986).*

I'm sure most of you have watched YouTube videos of people trying to hover a helicopter for the first time – it all looks easy for a few seconds until the aircraft drifts out of parameters and the quasi-pilot then moves one of the controls to correct the undesired motion only to find everything else changing at the same time. There are basically 3 controls to a helicopter: the cyclic stick positioned centrally (roughly) between one's legs which controls direction of lift produced by the spinning main rotor; the collective lever on our left hand side which controls the angle of attack of all the rotor blades in the main disk, and therefore the amount of lift being produced; and the pedals which apply or reduce the angle of attack of the tail rotor blades and so alter the torque being fed to the tail to counter the rotational forces produced by the spinning main rotor's drag. Changing power setting to alter the lift produced by the main rotor and hence the speed of flight or in this case the height of the hover affects the torque being fed through the main rotor shaft, which means the helicopter turns in the hover; putting in contra-pedal to stop the spin either increases or decreases the power demanded of the engine depending which way the rotor spins and which way the helicopter was turning and so the helicopter again moves upwards or downwards in an un-demanded manoeuvre! At the same time, it has probably started to drift forwards, backwards or sideways, and correcting this again upsets everything else! The helicopter makes bigger and bigger swings and ballooning movements until it is seemingly totally out of control. Annoyingly the instructor then takes over and within micro-seconds all is calm again and the helicopter back in a perfect hover exactly where it started from!

Helicopters, and particularly the Gazelle as it had no automatic flight or hover stabilisation devices, want to move all the time, and need constant small corrections to power for height or speed, heading and drift in order to stay in one place or one the desired path through the air. The secret is to make very small corrections nearly all of the time, catching any unwanted movement immediately it is detected.  The aim of all our training was to enable the flying to become almost automatic, so the good reconnaissance pilot could use the helicopter as a very fast recce vehicle, that means following the contours of the route being flown, far below the tops of the surrounding trees and often flying under power wires, even occasionally under bridges and telephone wires if necessary, often flying a whole mission well below 100' above the ground without really thinking about the physical aspect of actually flying it at all.  That meant he/she has the ability to be much more situationally aware from a safety point of view (not flying into wires and trees for instance and not over-flying an enemy position) and also to think about the tactical aspects of the task at hand with 100% of their brainpower – a very useful tool. Luckily for me, I was a very good seat of the pants helicopter pilot (probably gained during my gliding experience again), which eventually enabled me to operate the system to the maximum, in any terrain, and any weather and get the job done.  This was recognised throughout my career and rewarded with some very exciting postings later in my career where my skillset would prove highly useful both with the British Army and also with some foreign Armed Forces.  After many years' experience adding up to nearly 2,500 hours flying military helicopters I can still get in any helicopter and hold a steady hover almost without thinking about it.

However, that is jumping the gun somewhat – we are only just getting used to flying the Gazelle currently, and getting used to landing it in any situation we might find ourselves in including landing on a sloping bit of ground – for some reason 99% of the ground military pilots have to land on isn't flat tarmac – it's rough and hilly fields, desert sand, mountains or deep snow.  And occasionally the moving deck of a ship too!

One minor incident I'll remember for ever happened one rainy day when I was learning to land the Gazelle on the sloping ground training area, as it was called. The day started well with Mr Perrott and I going out and doing a few circuits. I had already gone solo on the Gazelle at this stage, so the pressure was ramping up a little as he introduced new manoeuvres and new situations to my flying almost daily. Landing on a slope in a helicopter is easy enough, if you do it right and if you stay within the limits set by the manufacturer – you can't just land on any old hillside. There is a

*Figure 12 - My first solo helicopter flight was in Gazelle "R - Romeo".*

down-slope limit, a sideways limit and an up-slope limit, which increase in severity in most single main rotor helicopters in that order – i.e. you can land on a steeper hill with the nose up than in any other direction. Land on too steep a sideways slope and the helicopter will roll over and down the hill; land nose down and the tail rotor can hit the ground rising behind you – with similarly catastrophic results. If the slope is too steeply up-hill the pilots will get an impressive first-hand view of the rotating main rotor blades hitting the hillside in front of the cockpit with the same result. To learn the techniques we have a 20m x 20m square laid out on the airfield (3 in fact) built up to around 2m above the surrounding ground with slopes on each side of varying severity across the 3 squares. This is the sloping ground training area, and it allows us to practice landing on progressively steeper ground, in all 3 slope directions and in any wind direction. The technique is to gently lower the Gazelle or any other skidded helicopter until the up-slope (for sideways landing) or forward tips of the skids for nose up landing just touch the ground where you want to land. Then, lowering the collective lever gently, we reduce power and hence lift slowly until the Gazelle drops enough for the bottom skid to touch the ground, drop the collective a bit more and the weight of the helicopter settles properly. All the time we are balancing the torque to the tail rotor to keep the helicopter straight and juggling the position of the cyclic to keep the helicopter exactly where we want it on the slope. Not so easy as it sounds – believe me. For the first few attempts the helicopter usually swerves sideways or slips down the hill or spins on the spot almost out of control as the student fights to keep pointing the right way and land exactly where he/she has been told to. After a few attempts it gets easier as we realise that looking well ahead and ignoring the instruments except for a check when the skids are almost fully on the ground to make sure we are "within limits" helps enormously. What happens if we ignore the limits – well, we can either chop the tail off, hit the blades into the bank above us or roll the helicopter down the slope – none very good for the helicopter or the occupants! Anyway, I was doing this just fine after my first few wandering attempts, and Mr Perrott decided I could cope on my own so he told me to land alongside the square or "sloping ground training area", and then got out and wandered off about 800m across the airfield to the instructor's office, from where no doubt he would keep a beady eye on me with a pair of binoculars! After a couple of reasonable attempts at landing it started to rain, so I landed and leant forwards to switch on the wipers. Only one worked, and it was on the left-hand side of the canopy, so my half of the screen wasn't being cleared of rain. I cycled the switch a couple of times, but "my" wiper refused to budge. By this time the whole of my side of the windscreen (canopy) was covered in running rainwater drops, and it was impossible to get a clear view out.

Later in my career I would simply take off and the wind passing the canopy would clear it, but here I couldn't do that as I hadn't been authorised to fly a circuit on my own. So, I did the only thing I could. I called the Air Traffic Control Tower and asked them to relay my problem to Mr Perrott sitting in the nice warm and dry instructor's crew-room to ask for instructions. *"Message passed – stay there"* was the answer I got back over the radio and after about 10 minutes a very wet Mr Perrott opened the left-hand door, leant in and flicked up the OTHER wiper switch! Arrgh, of course there were 2, one for each side, and I had forgotten. Off he went again getting even wetter and I completed the sortie and landed safely back on dispersal about 30 minutes later. That was very embarrassing! Amazingly he never mentioned it again, although nearly everyone else (civilian instructors, military instructors and my cohort of students) did of course!

One of the other evolutions we practiced a lot was engine failures. Most civilian helicopter pilots who have a PPLH (private Power licence helicopter) probably practice engine off landings once or twice in their flying careers. In the Army we practiced it at least once on most training sorties. Sometimes more often. If the engine stops on a single engine helicopter the pilot must lower the collective very quickly to let the collective clutch decouple the rotors from the engine or gearbox and keep spinning even though they are no longer being driven by the engine. Instead, the airflow through the rapidly descending helicopter's main rotor "disc" keeps the rotors turning, so that the helicopter can be manoeuvred safely albeit whilst descending very quickly to a safe (hopefully) landing site. The only time the pilot doesn't "dump" the collective lever is if the engine fails whilst the helicopter is in a hover close to the ground. Then the pilot maintains the collective pitch angle and the helicopter settles quickly onto the ground being cushioned by pulling the lever right up at the very last second. Once the collective lever has been "dumped" the rotors will speed up because of the airflow through them, and the pilot can fly the helicopter safely and under control until close to the ground when the aircraft is flared (pulling back on the cyclic to raise the nose) to increase the speed of the rotors and slow the helicopter down slightly, then a quick "check" short pull of the collective and levelling of the nose sets you up ready to cushion the impact with the ground by pulling the collective all the way up at he very last second. A safe landing can be achieved without damaging the helicopter at all in most engine failure scenarios as long as the pilot is in good practice and follows the drills correctly. Variations of this technique are learnt and practiced throughout military single engine helicopter training and later during every annual or 6 monthly check ride with a unit instructor. We learnt to complete safe landings from high-speed low level flight and high hovering flight as well as the slightly more benign in a settled cruise type of flying.

Having mastered sloping ground landings, the next week we found out that we were about to start learning to fly the Gazelle in Instrument Meteorological Conditions (IMC) – in the clouds to you or me. I mentioned going on "review" earlier when talking about Chipmunk flying. Unfortunately, the same process applied to basic helicopter flying and again to advanced helicopter flying which was still to come. Basic helicopter flying was the application of everything learnt on the Chipmunk to the Gazelle plus things like instrument flying – either in simulated cloud conditions or actually in the clouds. When it came to instrument flying, I stumbled. And how! The instrument flying syllabus covered around 5 hours of flying in simulated or real clouds culminating in an easy written and stringent flying exam, carried out by one of the senior instructors at Middle Wallop. Simulating flying in clouds didn't involve somehow making clouds appear, even though there were strong rumours around that time that the Russians could make clouds and accompanying heavy rain to order, and could therefore make an attack into Western Europe without fear of NATO air cover for the defending armies; it involved wearing a black folded contraction which clipped to our helmets and limited my field of vision to just the instrument panel inside the helicopter – I couldn't see the outside at all and so had to fly by referring only to what the instruments told me was going on and what the air traffic controller sitting at a radar somewhere was telling me to do over the civilian air to ground radio frequency – this harked back to being able to tell what attitude an aircraft was in by looking at the instruments during the pilot selection process when I was at Sandhurst. When instrument flying, one is expected to maintain heading, rate of turn, height and speed to within 10 degrees, 100 feet and 10 knots of the desired setting with a standard rate of turn at 3°/sec. All the time! Passing the physical test whilst keeping within these parameters was the aim and achieving this during a formal flying test meant being awarded a "White" Instrument rating – the minimum rating one had to have to fly in controlled airspace in peacetime. The basic, or White rating allowed us to make an approach under radar guidance down to the published airfield minimum altitude (agl[15]) plus 150'. That doesn't sound much but there were many months when the cloud-base at and around Middle wallop was less than that – meaning that we would not be allowed to practice IMC flying under those conditions without an instructor. Either the instructor or the air traffic controller would give instructions as to what height and what direction we should be flying in to remain safe and get to wherever we were heading to as well. I found this incredibly difficult and after 3 sorties was told that I wasn't good enough and was going to be put "on review". Shit!! We had already lost one student from our course of 9, and I didn't want to be the next.

I was allocated a new instructor - WO2 Dave A, a charming laid back and humorous expert pilot, and given a few extra hours to perfect my technique. I concentrated harder than I had ever done so in my whole life, but I still found it difficult: when noticing the speed dropping off and applying correction then I wouldn't notice the heading moving off the desired value until it had passed the maximum allowed variation, or the height would increase or decrease too much, and vice vera. I wasn't far off the required parameters, and never dangerous, but my flying just wasn't accurate enough. After 5 hours more instrument flying practice I failed my "end of review ride". I then had to go and have an interview with the Squadron Commander, Major Bob H, fully expecting to be told to pack my bags and leave – it was that simple.

Desperately holding back tears I listened to the Squadron

---

[15] Agl: above ground level. Another measure used is AMSL – above mean sea level which doesn't change with the terrain being flown over.

Commander being briefed by "Mr[16]" A who had taken me through the review period, and the examiner I had just flown with both say I wasn't good enough. I was asked to step out of the room for a few minutes. This was horrible, I expected to be called back in and told to go to the RTR or back to the REME, neither of which I really wanted to do. I simply wanted to fly. Amazingly, when I was called back in the Squadron Commander told me that I was to be given a second chance at review because the rest of my flying was pretty much flawless. This was unheard of, a second chance at "Review", and I saluted, about-turned and marched out of his office elated but also anxious (the first time I had ever been anxious about anything) about the next few hours flying. I knew that if I failed to make the grade I was done for.

After a sleepless weekend away from Middle Wallop I reported back to flying wing to see who I had been allocated to as instructor for what could be my final few hours flying as a quasi-military helicopter pilot. It was to be WO2 Ian R - an exceptionally experienced AAC pilot and excellent instructor. I had never flown with him before and he had a reputation as being calm and very fair, but to the book. Oh crikey!!

---

[16] In the Army officers called Warrant Officers (who had come up through the ranks from Private or Airtrooper in the AAC) "Mr". It was a mark of respect. Conversely, a commissioned officer being called "Mr" by an SNCO was not!

*Figure 13 - The Instrument Panel - our only reference when flying in cloud.*

Sitting in the Gazelle having started it up, "Mr" R walked out across the dispersal, climbed in and fastened his straps. I put the weird looking headgear on which limited my gaze to the instrument panel and nothing else. WO1 R told me that he would position the Gazelle in the right place on the airfield in the hover for me to execute an instrument take-off, simulating flying with clouds right down to ground level, and then hand control to me - I would initiate a climb out of the Instrument Departure Spot as if in the cloud already and then position the Gazelle under radar control into the Instrument Flying training area some 10 miles to the north of the airfield, where I would actually be in cloud. He watched me carefully though the flight for over an hour. I struggled to maintain the correct parameters whenever anything drifted off slightly, I would notice and correct it, but not quickly enough and therefore still fall foul of one or more of the other parameters being bust too. This wasn't going at all well.

After an hour WO1 R took control and told me to relax for a few minutes and he then asked me to explain how I was doing my "scan" of the instruments. The scan is a method of watching all the vital instruments in turn without fixating on any of them. This is required in order to be able to notice any drift off the required parameters (heading, rate of turn, height, speed and rate of climb remember) in time to be able to apply a correction before busting the limits. Amazingly, even though he could not see where my eyes were looking Mr R had realised that I was doing this incorrectly. Instead of looking at the most important instrument (the Attitude Indicator, known as the "AI" and in reality, an artificial horizon) for a few seconds then glancing at air speed, back to attitude indicator then to rate of turn, back to AI again etcetera, I was looking at each one in turn, only coming back to the AI once in each scan. That was my problem, and the other instructors hadn't picked up on it. How he knew that when we hardly moved our heads when instrument flying in order to concentrate on the instrument panel directly in front of us, I will never know; but I'm exceedingly grateful that he did. Such a simple mistake and it had nearly ruined my flying career before it had really started. Once he had worked out my problem, so I now knew I needed to scan from AI to each other instrument and then back to AI before looking at the next instrument I picked up any variation in desired heading, rate of turn, height, speed and rate of climb within milliseconds, and even learnt to concentrate on the AI most of the time as you could see from exactly where the aeroplane image was centred and whether it moved from the central spot whether anything was changing before it actually affected the aircraft enough to need correction. I started getting "blue" gradings (the best) for my instrument flying in simulated and in the cloud conditions and even got an overall "blue" for my subsequent end of review ride and instrument flying test[17]. I couldn't believe it – I was off review, back on track and loving it. I was so pleased to be told I'd also passed my final tactical handling check ride with the Chief flying Instructor at the end of Basic Rotary Wing.

After a few weeks' leave most of which I spent mountain walking in Scotland, we returned to Middle Wallop for the Advanced Rotary Phase. We had already passed the aviation medicine tests where we sat in a pressure chamber (depressurisation actually) and played kids games and tried to write our name whilst deprived of oxygen.

*Figure 15 - Middle Wallop Massed Approach.*

It was hilarious watching intelligent pilots who under hypoxia

---

[17] A few years later in my career I was able to maintain all required parameters within 5 degrees and 5 knots to be awarded my "Master Green" instrument rating – which I maintained for every flying tour through my career - almost unheard of for an officer pilot.

were not able to put a square shape in the correct hole in the standard kid's game and write illegibly whilst thinking we were doing a perfect job, eventually passing out momentarily at varying "heights" when the oxygen level dropped too much for us individually. We also went through dunker training which was more frightening for some. Here we were strapped into a mock-up of a helicopter and immersed in water to train us how to escape from the helicopter if we ever had to ditch in the sea or a lake.

This we did both from front seat and from the rear cabin many times, starting the right way up in daylight and ending upside down in the dark, following one's air bubbles to get out, remembering to grab something close to the doorway when the "helicopter" hit the water so we would know which way to go in the pitch-black upside-down under-water at night scenarios. This was my least favourite bit of the training, and we had to do it every 2 years throughout our flying career. It did teach me not to panic and to remain calmly strapped in until all motion had ceased, only then releasing our harness and swimming up to find the surface and breathe in some glorious air. Occasionally when placed in the rear cabin the pilots sitting closer to the rear door would take too long to get out and we would have to find a small air bubble in the back of the cabin and have a quick suck of breath before finding the exit in turn. I imagined that ditching and getting out from the front seat of a ditched Lynx helicopter equipped with armoured seats whilst wearing a heavy ceramic chest armour plate would be incredibly difficult.

Later in my career one army pilot was killed in the front seat of a ditched Lynx off the Croatian Coast and the other died trying to save the unconscious passengers in the back. Other Lynx crashes at sea resulted in a number of Royal Navy pilot deaths too. A sobering thought. Much later in my career, following these unfortunate accidents involving crashes into the sea AAC pilots and rear-crew were issued with STAS bottles (Short Term Air Supply) which allowed us to have a few short breaths underwater whilst sorting out the jumble of straps, communications leads and other paraphernalia we had to get rid of before being able to exit the aircraft underwater.

The Advanced Rotary Phase was taught as if each flight was a military mission – "orders[18]" were given, and a task followed which had been designed to teach us some aspect of flying as a job in the field army. All the missions were flown with a very experienced military instructor sitting in the left hand (non-handling) seat. I flew mostly with WO1 R and with WO1 M – who later on my career would fly a Lynx attached to my Squadron in Bosnia. After each flight we had a military and a flying debrief – the grading colours and review system very much still being applied for both tactical aspects and the physical handling of the helicopter too.

It was great fun, flying very low, often inches above the ground following contours dipping down into folds of the landscape to prevent the "enemy" from seeing us, hopping over hedges, between trees and under power wires. This was a particularly exciting evolution, and contrary to what you see in movies was usually done at fast walking pace crossing very close to a pylon so we knew we could squeeze through beneath the wires – it was

---

[18] Orders: Situation, Mission, Execution, Sustainment, Command & Control: a standard format used throughout the Army to ensure everyone knew what was going on and what effect (on the enemy usually, but it could also be used when providing assistance to civilians or another body) was desired by their bosses and those at least one level above too.

notoriously difficult to judge the height of the wires above the spinning rotor, especially at night when using Night Vision Goggles, which we learnt when NVG was introduced later in my career. Crossing under wires and other obstacles was a vital skill as in Germany during the Cold War era NATO jets flew at around 250 feet above the terrain, and we in helicopters needed to deconflict by always remaining below 150 feet above the terrain (50'agl). Wires in Germany usually extended to either 200' or 300' above the surrounding terrain so we had to fly under them. We learnt how to fly in Nuclear Biological and Chemical clothing and masks and to fly tactically at night but without night vision goggles which were yet to be cleared for helicopter flying, and how to evade enemy fighter aircraft and attack helicopters and how to control live artillery gunfire out on the Salisbury Plain training ranges. During this phase we also learnt how to land in confined areas. This usually meant landing in a small clearing in the middle of a wooded area, but it could also mean landing close to buildings, or on a ship where the rotors were passing close to an obstruction which would cause the helicopter to crash if impacted. The technique was a little more involved than that employed by the US Army or Marine Corps in Vietnam! Unlike the Huey and Cobras, the rotor system of a Gazelle and most of the other UK armed forces helicopters is pretty delicate and impacting the spinning rotor blade on anything was likely to end up with the helicopter wrapping itself around the obstacle and ending up in one hell of a mess. So, we had to be careful and make sure there was always some clearance between the blade tips and the obstructing object. Landings in confined areas therefore always began with a recce over and around the selected site. We were looking for clearings in the woods which had the following attributes: size – big enough; surface wind – so which way might we have to approach the clearing before letting down into it in a hover; slope – within limits for nose up or skid up or sideways slope landings; surrounds – no obstructions on the way in, or the way we were likely to have to fly out, or inside the clearing on the way down and on the ground – it wouldn't do to land on a big log for instance or have a rotor tip hit a branch which stuck out into the clearing a bit more than the rest; stock – no animals who might move unexpectedly or be scared by the noise of the helicopter; surface - not too rough, preferably solid, no semi-hidden obstacles etcetera. After confirming the above during the recce, the technique was to fly a pretty level approach descending gently to come to a hover over the area chosen for landing, then position the helicopter so that the tail and main rotor were clear of branches before starting to reduce power gently lowering into the hole in the trees. We chose a forward and a sideways marker because once we started to descend and were surrounded by trees it would become very difficult to pick up any unwanted movement of the helicopter until it was too late, especially in small clearings, and the blades hit the trees. Keeping the forward and sideways markers in the same position relative to the helicopter would show us that we were not drifting forwards or backwards or to one side or the other – all very important to ensure we stayed in the middle of the selected clearing. All the while our head was on a swivel looking out for obstacles and obstructions on the way down. When we got to the bottom of the clearing, we would always carry out a sloping ground landing procedure because it was impossible to tell exactly what slope we were hovering over with a lack of horizontal references, and we didn't really have time to be able to look into the cockpit to check where the AI showed the horizon to be. Once down we could shut down if needed. Taking off again involved using the same references and if there was room in the clearing, having a look over our tail by spinning the helicopter through 90 degrees in the hover before climbing to tree top level. Of course, sometimes there wasn't room so the safest thing to do was to have a look whilst hovering at tree top level as if the treetops were at ground level before flying away in a powered climb gaining flying speed as quickly as reasonably possible to allow autorotation if the engine stopped. All helicopters suffer from a safe flying limitation called "dead man's curve"; this is a pictorial representation of how much height is needed under the helicopter at all airspeeds from hovering to the maximum, for the pilot to be able to stop the helicopter descending and fly way before hitting the ground if the single engine fails (or one engine fails in a twin-engine machine). Whilst in the hover during tactical military flying the height needed is often a lot more than that which is actually available, so effectively we fly knowing that we will crash should the engine /one engine fail. Sitting in a hover over trees is a typical example of this, and something we would do a lot in Germany during the Cold War, but doing this when climbing out of a confined area was another. We minimised time spent in the dead man's curve whenever flying but accepted that as military pilots the tactical situation would over-ride the simple elements of flying safety that a good non-military pilot should follow.

*Figure 14 - Air OP Gunnery Training - author front centre.*

Air OP Gunnery training came next – learning to control up to a Division's worth of artillery using the Gazelle as a target spotter and then adjusting fire to maximise the impact of the artillery strike. This was fun, especially the live round test at the end of the training and being brought under effective artillery fire for real whilst looking out of a specially built bunker on Salisbury plain through 150mm thick glass plating. Direct hits by some of the shrapnel broke a few layers of the glass in front of us but thankfully didn't penetrate all the way through – it would have been a rather messy and expensive end to our careers!

One of my cohort, a charming and experienced infantry Captain now started to struggle. Captain Paul R had already been on review during Basic Rotary, and now went on review a further 3 times during the advanced rotary phase. The pressure was relentless. Unfortunately, he was "chopped" a week from the end of the course – very sad for him and demoralising for the rest of us as we had got to know him incredibly well during the last year's intensive training. Finally, the FHTs (Final Handing Checks) came and went – out of 8 officers and 2 soldiers 2 had fallen by the wayside, one potential AAC officer[19] deciding he didn't like helicopter flying at the beginning of basic rotary, and one being chopped days from the end of the complete course. We had been taught and tested and found not wanting. After a magnificent day where we paraded in front of our families and were presented with our Army Helicopter Wings in the AAC museum, we were badged Army Helicopter Pilots and were all about to be posted to our first operational units.

---

[19] He had to rebadge to another Arm and became a Royal Signals officer.

# Chapter 7

## First Flying Posting – 3 Regt AAC – Gazelle - Soest, Germany.

Following the year spent training as a helicopter pilot at Middle Wallop in Hampshire I was posted to Soest in Germany as a Gazelle reconnaissance pilot. My tour there lasted from 07 January 1987 until 17 January 1989, and I spent nearly 8 months on detachment to Northern Ireland during the tour. Shortly after arriving I found out that 2 of my soldiers from my 1 QLR infantry platoon had been killed during their tour of Belfast – I always wondered if I could have done anything more to help avoid their deaths, but of course could never find out.

Soon after arrival in Soest I qualified as a BAOR[20] aircraft commander which meant I understood the rules concerning flying in the Cold War period in BAOR Germany and could get around the country without (a) getting too lost and (b) accidentally crossing the border into communist East Germany thereby causing a major diplomatic incident. One morning I was in the control tower at Soest gathering weather and route information for a flying task later in the day and idly watched a Lynx containing Sgt T and Cpl B with WO2 Strachan, Lt Griffiths and another as passengers, as it took off and departed to the North, en-route I think, to the UK to go and collect another Lynx which had been in major servicing. As I watched it fly over the village of Schallern approximately one kilometer to the North of the airfield I saw it plunge downwards behind some trees and did not see it climb back to normal operating height. Something made me realise it had a serious problem and I told the Ops Warrant Officer to hit the crash alarm pointing out

---

[20] BAOR – British Army of the Rhine Germany – the stationing of British Army units in Germany to deter the USSR from launching an attack into Europe during, and after the Cold war.

the location of the Lynx, ran downstairs and leapt into my car. Less than a couple of minutes later, guided by the rapidly rising plume of smoke, I arrived at the crash site to help the 3 passengers crawling out of the back of the wrecked Lynx, with the 2 pilots surrounded by flames struggling in the cockpit. Sadly, neither managed to escape. A German photographer took the brunt of my anger, he was taking explicit photos of the 2 pilots, and I ripped the camera from his hands and exposed the film he had been taking of the 2 crew in their last moments, moments which are permanently etched into my brain. Although Major Malcolm Braithwaite, the AAC doctor attached to the Regiment, told me afterwards that the pilots were killed on impact and were not burned alive I didn't believe him as the cockpit area didn't appear to be badly damaged enough to have killed them. I still had those images very strongly embedded in my brain and did not discuss the accident again - in those days no-one talked about such things, and so the seeds of a PTSD mental breakdown presumably continued inexorably germinating in my sub-consciousness.

One of the big changes in the way the Army operated its helicopters at the time I started flying them was to move from a pilot and aircrewman basis to the 2 pilot system where both front seats would normally be occupied by qualified pilots, the left hand seat by a senior pilot known as the aircraft commander who was in command of the helicopter, and a less experienced pilot whose prime purpose was to fly the helicopter (flying from the right hand seat) and allow the aircraft commander to concentrate on "fighting" the helicopter as a very fast and agile weapons and intelligence gathering platform.

I was lucky. Being on the first P2 course at Middle Wallop I expected to have to be the right-hand seat pilot to a more experienced SNCO or officer aircraft commander for a while, but then arrived in Germany whilst aircrew manning in the rapidly expanding Army Air Corps hadn't caught up. I would spend most of my first 3 years actually flying from the right-hand seat with a crewman in the left. This meant my hands-on flying experience was phenomenal, something which wasn't the case for those qualifying a few years later. The plan was that P2 soldier pilots would spend a few years learning the ropes before becoming aircraft commanders, officers would take command after 6 months to a years' experience in a flying unit, but due to the shortage I (and 3 others from my pilot's course) was asked to attend the aircraft commanders' course back at Middle Wallop within a few months of arriving in Germany.

*Figure 17 - My Aircraft Commander's Course (author front right).*

This was a mission heavy course with sorties being planned as before but flown as an aircraft commander from the left-hand seat where we could access the Gazelle Observation Aid (GOA) a roof mounted gyro-stabilised sight. In the Gazelle flying from the left-hand seat could be a slight problem as the instrument panel was placed off-set in front of the right-hand seat P2 and the view of some instruments for the left-hand seat aircraft commander was obscured and suffered from parallax errors[21]. This wasn't too much of an issue in tactical flight when most pilots spent the vast amount of their time looking out through the canopy, but when it came to instrument flying (needed in the clouds) it could be problematic. On top of that the left-hand cyclic stick was very off-set to the left and the collective was at an unusual angle compared with the right-hand seat set, and was missing a couple of important buttons. Of course, we had to fly to the same exacting standards from the disadvantaged left-hand seat as we did from the right seat during our training.

Luckily Mr R had done his job exceedingly well, and I transferred my right-hand seat instrument flying skills to the left-hand seat with no issues. Others didn't! Anyway, the lack of pilots manning the AAC ensured that I spent most of my time actually flying the Gazelle, with an aircrewman in the left hand seat, and this experience initially flying tactically at very low level in Germany and then not long later flying a vast number of hours in Northern Ireland set me up incredibly well for more testing flying to come in the Lynx and other bigger helicopters in the future. We often flew

---

[21] Parallax errors occur when an instrument designed to looked at from straight in front of it is viewed from a position well to the side. The needle (in those days all instruments had needles – there were no digital instruments or moving maps) looked like it was over-reading when it was vertical at the top of its arc, under-reading at the bottom and only read "true" when horizontal across the instrument face.

the Gazelle at 120 knots (240 Km/h or 140mph) literally a few feet above the ground in Germany particularly when crossing open ground between two tree lines of areas of scrub. This was very exciting especially as the canopy at the front of the Gazelle wraps around under our seats and so the effect was very similar to riding a motorbike fast, or perhaps a broomstick! When turning the helicopter, the edge of the spinning rotor disk would be only a few feet above the grass or hedges and we learnt to execute "quick-stops"[22] effortlessly very low to the ground, before creeping up to a ridgeline to peep over before speeding off again.

When close to "the enemy" we would sometimes land on the reverse slope in dead ground to the "enemy" before getting out of the Gazelle, initially running up and then crawling to the crest with a pair of binoculars to scout out the ground ahead. This reduced the risk of our position being compromised inadvertently. I would often head out with a second Gazelle (usually commanded by my second in command) to confirm previous recces in the finger valleys – a large area south of Hildesheim where invading Soviet tanks would be forced to follow a set of valleys in the advance toward the Ruhr and the known crossing points for tank bridges over the Weser river, and in the Einbeck bowl a large open area where I could use my airborne forward air controller skills to the maximum. Flying very low, one Gazelle would fly down the valleys slowly a few inches above the ground replicating the path and speed

---

[22] Quick-stops were practiced as an exercise at 50' agl. They involved either flaring the helicopter first to start slowing down then turning quite aggressively into the prevailing wind or turning into the wind then flaring aggressively to come to a stop quickly whilst maintaining a height above the ground as close to 50' as possible. During tactical flying the manoeuvre was carried out at a lower height if the tactical scenario required it, rotor disk only a few feet from the ground.

of advancing tanks. The other would find and sit in observation positions, often hovering in a depression over trees in the dead man's curve, watching their progress along the envisaged route, whilst the first Gazelle tried to spot them. If they could not then the observation position was deemed viable, and a covered route into and out of the position worked out. Covered could mean physically behind a rise in the ground but could also mean in full sight of the enemy but unable to be seen because of the background behind the moving Gazelle providing camouflage. We had to be very aware of the direction to the sun as the glint off the spinning rotor disk could easily give away our position if the wrong angles were achieved. The aim during any enemy advance by massed armour was to be able to bring down artillery fire onto them as they entered the killing zone, to force their commanders to sit inside their turrets where their visibility was seriously reduced and then use anti-tank missiles fired by Lynx helicopters and infantry Milan teams to destroy them, very similar tactics to those we have recently seen used in Ukraine.

There was an issue with doing quick stops when the Gazelle was close to its maximum all up mass. Loss of tail rotor authority could occur, and this was blamed on the helicopter being handled badly - i.e. poor flying by the pilot. At the time no-one was quite sure what triggered the loss of control, but it was thought that turning left rather than right could provoke the unwanted result – spinning round and round out of control. One day I executed a quick stop and did indeed turn left to slow down – I had to as there were trees along my right-hand side. Without warning the tail spun out to the right and I completed around 2 full spins before I got the helicopter back under control. Luckily, I was far enough away from the tree line and over reasonably level ground and managed somehow to not hit anything whilst careering out of control a few feet above the ground.

*Figure 15- East German Troops watching us watching them...*

On another occasion I remember flying across the exercise area close to Fallingbostel in Northern Germany at very low level whilst pushing forwards to identify some "enemy" vehicles which were advancing towards the Rhine – the usual scenario for exercises in the days when we thought the Russians were going to invade NATO territory. The lane cut through the trees I was flying down was about 20m across – plenty of room to fly slowly down and be able to turn around to exit the observation position without climbing and giving my position away. The aim was to get my crewman, who was operating the GOA, into such a position as just the rotor and the GOA lens was visible to the enemy position so that he could positively identify them without us being seen. Tick tick tick... Oh bugger, that was the tips of the blades hitting the surrounding trees. Unlike the Huey flown by US Army pilot Robert Mason in Chickenhawk (one of the best books about flying helicopters ever) the blades on a Gazelle are quite fragile and hitting trees could result in the blades coming apart. I landed and inspected the blade tips. One of the sacrificial tips used to set the tracking level of each blade was slightly scratched but the others were just fine. There was obviously no further damage to my trained engineer's eye, so I got back in and flew on, reporting the scratch later to the engineers.

*Figure 16 – Two of my Gazelles with Anti-Tank Lynx TOW at 5 minutes NTM.*

The most frightening incident occurred during another exercise in the Einbeck Bowl area. My crewman at the time, Cpl Dave Redwood (Parachute Regiment), and I were flying forward of most of the defending troops calling in A10 Thunderbolt ground attack aircraft in simulated strikes against the advancing enemy armour. Running down on fuel we decided to nip back to a Forward Arming and Refueling Point (FARP) for a suck of avgas. I was flying down the right-hand edge of a long wood-line in one of the "finger valleys" at ultra-low level a few feet off the ground and at about 120 knots. Dave was map reading whilst I concentrated on the ground ahead. He had the map slightly up in front of him obscuring my view around my 10-o-clock when I heard him say *"go right"*. I thought he was directing me where to fly to our next bound so aimed the Gazelle slightly right of our track. Then Dave said *"GO right"* with more emphasis. I had just enough time to think WTF when he shouted, *"GO F***ING RIGHT!"*. I reckon all this took less than 2 seconds. Realising that something was amiss I put the Gazelle on its right "wingtip" and pulled hard. Through the plexiglas canopy I saw an Alouette helicopter fly across our line of flight about 2 rotors disk diameters away. We missed her, and yes it was either her or a very pretty long-haired male pilot clearly visible as we were missed hitting them by milliseconds. They didn't look right or left as they popped out of the wood-line just ahead of us and to this day I don't think they had a clue how close they and we came to ending up in a mangled fireball strewn across the West German countryside.

The weather could be very unpredictable in Germany in the Winter, on one occasion the whole Regiment was out on exercise and my Squadron (I was the Gazelle Flight commander with 6 Gazelle, and there was a Lynx flight commander with 6 Lynx, one of which was normally flown by the Officer commanding the Squadron) was moving location when we flew into some freezing rain. I was leading the squadron towards its new location flying semi-tactically at around 100' agl (remember the fast jets were cleared down to 250' agl at all times) under an 8/8ths cloudy sky. There was no warning; freezing rain occurs when the airframe temperature of the Gazelle or Lynx (or any other aircraft) is well below zero degrees Celsius and it flies into some super-cooled rain which can be as light as drizzle or as heavy as that found in a thunderstorm. The super-cooled water instantly turns to ice on the below zero surfaces which in this case was everything – the rotor blades the fuselage and the canopy. Immediately we flew into the very light rain the canopy went from being a completely clear bubble all around me to being totally opaque in about 3 seconds. I could not see a thing and we were flying at around 100 knots just 100' above undulating ground. Shit!! Thinking very fast I punched the Gazelle's left-hand rudder pedal[23] hard to turn the nose quickly to the left. Going left also increased the power available to me if I needed a boost as the torque required from the engine to power the tail rotor was lessened when turning left. I warned the following aircraft over the radio to turn away immediately and lined up the side window which I nearly always had open for fresh air whilst I was flying and was able to see enough out through the small aperture (approx. 15cm x 10cm) and use my instrument flying skills to safely slow down, descend and land in deep snow without damaging the aircraft. Calling to say we were safely down on the UHF radio I heard my whole flight say they were landing before they hit the freezing rain, and then the Squadron commander also said the Lynx crews were attempting a landing. Nothing more was heard from his Lynx. I walked over to the nearest farm and asked (I spoke quite good German by this stage) to use their phone as there were no mobile phones in use back in 1987. Reporting our issue to the Brigade HQ I advised that we were stuck for the night as it was getting very dark, and that we had not heard from the Squadron commander's Lynx since his emergency call. I learnt later that the Brigade gave him another 90 minutes to find a phone and then mobilised 3 infantry battalions to search for his presumably crashed helicopter through the night. Apparently, he was found

---

[23] There is no "rudder" in a helicopter but varying the torque fed to the tail rotor or the pitch of the tail rotor blades is affected by using the "rudder" pedals.

tucked up in his sleeping bag in the back of his safely landed Lynx a few cold dark hours later, you can imagine what the poor infantry thought wading around in approximately 3 feet of freezing snow all night. The lesson learnt was to always make maximum effort to pass messages when in trouble. One perk of the job (as if we needed one zooming around Germany at ultra-low level) was being able to land alongside the small roadside stores called "Bratty" stands or "Imbis" to stock up on the delicious grilled bratty sausages and chips and a coffee or a lamb pitta bread whenever we were peckish!

On one memorable occasion we took part in a fire-power demonstration for some visiting European troops. We recced a route which they could see us flying along a river valley and under a railway bridge arch – around twice the width of the Lynx rotor disk. We did this at some speed having practiced a lot – it must have looked very cool to see 2 Gazelle and 6 Lynx fly under this seemingly tiny bridge and it was certainly exciting from the cockpit!

On another sortie, during a major exercise called "REFORGER" I was calling in fast-air ("smoky Joe" Phantom 4 and the A10 Thunderbolt) from the German and American air forces to simulate dropping bombs against "enemy armour" emerging from woods and trying to force a crossing on the Weser river. To do this I spent around an hour at a time hovering just above the water in the middle of a canal as it was the only place I could find enough cover so that only my sighting system was visible to the approaching "enemy" armoured vehicles. It was very exciting, and we had to keep an extra look-out sideways occasionally moving out of the way of approaching gigantic river barges which the Germans used to move coal into the Ruhr factories! Exercise REFORGER was the major exercise which took place once every 4 years to test the American's ability to deploy

20,000 plus troops over the Atlantic, and for German, British and Dutch troops to hold back the advancing "enemy" long enough for those American troops to arrive, collect their tanks and artillery vehicles from storage and get into defensive positions before the "enemy" crossed the Weser River. It would be unheard of today but there was a tally placed on the number of soldiers who could be killed accidentally before the exercise was called off. Rumour had it that the tally was 12. On this occasion 4 unfortunate soldiers lost their lives when they decided to sleep under their tank (as it was warmer there) and unfortunately the tank sank into the boggy ground during the night crushing them. A number of other soldiers died in road traffic accidents, but the exercise wasn't called off early.

# Chapter 8.

## Northern Ireland – Back-to-Back Emergency Tour.

A tour based in Northern Ireland followed, actually it was 2 short or what was known as "emergency" tours back-to-back. I was due to go for a 4-month stint based in Aldergrove but flying mainly over Belfast city out of Palace barracks, Hollywood, in Belfast City; but ended up going 4 months early due to my predecessor being ill, and then staying for my original tour too. During the second half of my tour the Adjutant (the CO's right-hand man) had to spend some time away from the unit, and I was asked to stand up into his shoes for a while whenever I wasn't actually flying. This was good experience for me and helped enormously in a subsequent tour where my Commanding Officer and I (then serving as his Adjutant) were asked to set up an airmobile aviation Regiment from scratch. Most of my flying was as a solo pilot with an observer – a corporal usually, siting in the left-hand seat.

Sitting in the right-hand seat of the Gazelle I got a lot of hands-on flying – sometimes in horrendous wintry weather, and built up over 600 hours experience over Belfast, where I spent much time hovering on various tasks, and around South Armagh. We were called out virtually every night to support the RUC and Army troops patrolling the streets, roads and fields due to the number of bombs, shootings, sniper attacks and intimidation of civilians occurring at the time. Almost none of this activity reached the press in the UK mainland – it hardly ever did, and yet here were British citizens and soldiers being subjected to lethal violence nearly every day of their lives. Most of this first part of the tour involved high level hovering over the city of Belfast with occasional landings in some of the fortified barracks located around the city.

My Gazelle was equipped with various aids for use by the observer in the left-hand seat which allowed us to fly out of small arms range whilst watching suspects mostly without them being aware of us. Occasionally the high pitch whine of the Gazelle's engine could be heard at street level, but we were difficult to spot hovering very high above and it would have been impossible for someone on the ground to know they were being picked out for close observation. I flew with LCpls B and D[24] mostly – both superb aircrewmen whose task was to navigate for me and operate the "night-sun" searchlight and onboard observation systems. Like most pilots, I taught both the rudiments of helicopter flying so that if I were incapacitated by being shot, they might have a chance of landing the Gazelle reasonably safely in a barracks or at Aldergrove airfield. I did the same with my crewmen in BAOR, so they could land in a German farmers field if necessary. We worked mostly with a Royal Scots colour sergeant on the ground during this tour and we got to know each other very well, he learning he could depend on me for first class intelligence concerning movement of undesirables around his men's positions during their patrols around the Whiterock and Miltown areas of Belfast in particular.

On one occasion I was flying from Aldergrove to Palace Barracks in very poor weather – low cloud and foggy. I passed very close over the top of a power pylon near the village of Nutts' Corner about halfway between the 2 locations and apparently the power went off locally seconds later. A friendly local rang the airfield to say he thought I might have hit the wires and crashed but he couldn't see me because of the fog! When I landed at Palace

---

[24] Often JNCO aircrewmen were subsequently recommended for pilot training when they made Corporal rank. Unfortunately, LCpl D (by then a WO2 and an aircraft commander in his own right) was killed in a helicopter crash on 18th May 1999 along with 2 others when a Lynx helicopter he was flying in suffered an engine fire and crashed during the attempted engine off /autorotation landing.

approximately 10 minutes later the World had gone mad. I immediately called the ops room on the phone and told them I was perfectly okay and that "no I hadn't hit any wires en-route"! The Regimental Instructor decided that I must have done so and told me to drive back to Aldergrove to face the music. Before I did, with my pistol tucked under my seat, I checked the Gazelle over very carefully. I was a qualified and experienced engineer, remember, and I knew what marks I should be looking for if I had physically hit or caused an electrostatic discharge to jump to my helicopter from the high-tension power wires. There were no marks of any kind. As I drove back to Aldergrove via some of the most dangerous streets for a British soldier in the World, a REME team were gathered and eventually flown to Palace Barracks to inspect the Gazelle before it could be allowed to fly again. Why I couldn't wait and fly back with them, if there was any damage, or continue my duties if there wasn't I'll never know. On arriving at Aldergrove I met with the regimental helicopter instructor who briefed me to fly the same route with him in the other front seat, so we could see whether my route selection was safe or not considering the poor weather. He said he would sign the Gazelle out (each flight we read through the F700 engineering record book to check the aircraft was serviceable, equipped with any special kit we needed and sign to say we understood which bits of the aircraft weren't working properly - a regular occurrence for non-safety related items) and he would then join me flying from the left hand "aircraft commander's" seat. I walked out to the aircraft about 90 minutes after leaving Belfast and climbed in – there were no controls in the left hand pilot position, so when the regimental helicopter instructor climbed in he was pretty surprised as he would usually fly with a set of controls so he could take over and demonstrate something if he wanted to, and it was unusual for a pilot to fly in any front seat without a set of controls for safety reasons. His surprise meant he hadn't read the F700 properly and this was supposed to be an official check ride – so to cover his embarrassment he told me to take off and fly the route anyway. Having shown him the pylon we then got a message that the REME team could find no evidence of damage to my Gazelle sitting on the ground in Palace Barracks, so I was told to fly back there where I landed and got out then he flew the second Gazelle back. What a FUBAR[25] as the US Marines would say!

During the second 4 months I worked both over Belfast and also around the infamous Northern/Southern Ireland border areas based mostly at Bessbrook Mill – at the time the busiest heliport in the UK, guiding soldiers on the ground particularly in South Armagh, then one of the most lawless parts of the UK since the Dark Ages. I would use my thermal imaging video camera to search for insurgents and potential ambushes against the infantry patrols; providing much needed moral support to those engaged in a battle of wills, and sometimes armed fight with terrorists at very close quarters. Flying up and down from Bessbrook on the border with Southern Ireland was fun flying, almost always carried out at high speed and low level in order to reduce the likelihood of an insurgent being able to target us effectively with small arms as we flew over. Keeping to contours and below treetops was fun in capitals although we did have to learn the location of every set of wires enroute as there wasn't time to sit reading the map when flying solo at low level.

I spent considerable time flying in support of troops in the hunt for extremists and their weapons. I remember flying a sergeant one day, doors removed from the Gazelle so that he and his mate could sit across the cockpit armed with sniper rifles pointing out both

---

[25] FUBAR: F**ked Up Beyond All Repair!

sides of the aircraft. We were hovering around the area between Divis & the Black Mountain and Dundrod at ultra-low level for ages, and I was getting more and more concerned we were presenting a good target to any IRA sniper lurking nearby. Eventually I asked the sergeant what we were doing, and he said *"making ourselves a target for a suspected sniper"* – luckily, he must have been lurking elsewhere!

On 16th March 1988 I was hovering above Milltown Cemetery in Belfast providing overwatch whilst the funeral of 3 IRA members rumoured in the popular Press to have been killed by the SAS in Gibraltar a few weeks before went on beneath us. An individual called Michael Stone[26] decided to throw a number of grenades at the mourners and I was able to track him from the air eventually talking the RUC onto his hiding place in the garden of a terrace house near Divis Flats. Whilst shopping in Belfast in civvies[27] a few days after the Milltown Cemetery incident we noticed a TV playing in the shop we were in, and on it saw 2 men

---

[26] The Milltown Cemetery attack (also known as the Milltown Cemetery killings or Milltown massacre) took place on 16 March 1988 at Milltown Cemetery in Belfast, Northern Ireland. During the large funeral of three Provisional IRA members killed in Gibraltar, an Ulster Defence Association (UDA) member, Michael Stone, attacked the mourners with hand grenades and pistols. He had learned there would be no police or armed IRA members at the cemetery. As Stone then ran towards the nearby motorway, a large crowd chased him, and he continued shooting and throwing grenades. Three people had been killed and more than 60 wounded. The "unprecedented, one-man attack" was filmed by television news crews and caused shock around the world.

[27] We were allowed to go into areas of Belfast and the surrounding countryside as long as we didn't enter any especially dangerous areas such as the Falls Road.

who we later found out were Royal Signals corporals[28] being dragged out of their car and murdered during an IRA funeral which was being broadcast live, only a few hundred metres away from the shop – not a pleasant experience.

*Figure 20 - Bessbrook Helipad - a VERY busy Landing Site.*

I nearly ran out of fuel one night – we were supporting the Royal Scots who were coming under a lot of sniper fire and had been bombed too during my sortie. I stretched the time I could stay in support until the fuel warning light came on – which generally meant 40kg of fuel left (which should give us 10 minutes of usable fuel) and then hung on a few minutes more as they were actually

---

[28] Cpl David Howes and Cpl Derek Wood, both Royal Signals.

"in contact[29]" on the ground withdrawing to Whiterock Barracks. As soon as they were safely inside the barracks I turned and headed off across Belfast towards Palace barracks which was exactly 4 minutes flying time away at full speed. As I passed over the yellow Harland & Wolff cranes at Belfast docks the rapidly flashing fuel warning light changed to solid yellow. This meant I had 10 kgs of fuel left – only 4 minutes flight to completely empty the tank and only if I remained in level flight. This was below legal military limits and meant I could experience a flame-out any second due to having to bank the aircraft round to make an approach and then flare to slow down close to the landing site. Somehow, I made it. When the young airtrooper fueled the Gazelle for me shortly afterwards he told me he put 336 kilograms of fuel in. A full tank is only 340 kilograms, so it had been a very close shave. He changed the fuel tanker log, so it looked like he had put 326 kilograms in and nothing more was said – just a very sweaty AAC Captain thinking he'd never do that again!

One wintery evening I was flying back into Palace Barracks after finishing a round robin task landing in a few of the high walled security compounds spread around the worst areas of Belfast. LCpl D was in the left-hand seat looking at the map when there was an almighty crash… we had collided with a big seagull which had come through the perspex or plexiglas canopy, just in front of my yaw control pedals and was now flapping wildly around the cockpit covering us with blood and feathers. LCpl D managed to catch the bird and break its neck, there was no way we could put it out through the door alive at height over the city – it might have killed

---

[29] "In Contact" means the enemy, whoever they are, are actively engaging you, usually with rifle or machinegun fire, but it applies to any form of attack.

someone on the ground!

On another occasion I vaguely felt a very high frequency vibration start to come up through the yaw control pedals whilst in a high hover over central Belfast. After a few seconds I decided that it was probably an engine problem (that engineering training again), and that it appeared to be getting worse. Declaring an emergency on the civilian and military radios – the latter in case I had an engine failure and had to land in Belfast where we would instantly become high value targets to the IRA, I headed at height towards Aldergrove airport. Having declared an emergency, I had priority and Aldergrove turned away a civilian airliner to allow me to continue at height until I was almost over the airfield boundary – this to give me time to autorotate into a safe landing if the engine failed en-route. I elected to make a powered approach to the runway edge at a speed where I could instantly convert the powered approach to an engine off autoration if necessary. Thankfully we landed safely and immediately shut the engine down. The Gazelle was towed into the REME workshop, and I waited to see what the engineers thought. Had I acted precipitately, should I have ignored the vibration, was I right to have declared the emergency which closed down Aldergrove airport for 20 minutes all went through my mind. After a little while the REME warrant officer in charge of maintaining the Gazelles came into the crew room and came straight over and shook my hand. He said they reckoned the engine would have seized solid in the next 5 minutes, so my actions had just saved the engine, and possibly the aircraft, my passenger and myself! I learnt to go with my sixth sense from this incident and rely on my engineering knowledge telling me things weren't right through the rest of my flying life.

The tour continued with almost daily call-out after call-out, usually at night and on top of my daily tasking supporting the infantry and PSNI / RUC[30] in Belfast or on the border with Southern Ireland due to bombs, shootings and rioting. In the 8 months I flew in Northern Ireland I managed to fly almost 700 hours in command of the Gazelle in some of the most interesting and testing flying of my career, or so I thought at the time; I hadn't been exposed to arctic or tactical flying in mountainous terrain at that time.

*Figure 21 - Lynx Shot Down by PIRA.*

Towards the end of my extended tour, a Lynx with 2 crew I knew very well was shot down by the PIRA, something we always had in the back of our minds; but luckily after a sustained chase and firefight on the ground after managing a safe if rather hurried

---

[30] PSNI / RUC – the Police Service in Northern Ireland / Royal Ulster Constabulary

landing, they were rescued. The crew were both Royal Navy pilots attached to my Germany based AAC Regiment and the officer amongst them was mercilessly ribbed for months due to the fact that he would never leave the base area when off duty (something we were allowed to do in civvies, remember) because he always "felt" he was going to be targeted. In the end he was right I guess, but it was whilst in uniform carrying out his duties flying!

# Chapter 9.

***B*ack to Germany.** Returning after 8 months away to BAOR and 3 Regiment AAC based in Soest I had a superb couple of years as Gazelle Flight commander, flying mostly with LCpl F and Cpl Dave Redwood (both attached to the AAC from the Parachute regiment) spending many hours zooming at low level around the BAOR area reconnoitering Lynx fire positions against the potential Russian advance into Germany – my prime role was to act as a reconnaissance pilot finding suitable sites where the Lynx could loiter safely out of site before popping up to fire their anti-tank missiles, then lead the Lynx groups in and out of those positions, calling down artillery on the invading tank formations to make them close down[31] – which made it much harder for them to spot our forces. I also learnt to control fast jet ground attack aircraft and qualified as an airborne forward air controller (ABFAC) and eventually a Supervisory ABFAC (able to supervise other ABFACs continuation training) whilst honing my skills flying day and night throughout Germany. Most of the fixed wing jet aircraft were Phantom F4 known as "Smoky Joes" because they left contrails of burnt fuel behind them when on re-heat, or A10 "Warthogs" of the USAF. This was such fun and a real eye-opener as to what my secondary task might be should the Russians decide to invade Western Germany. Due to the Cold War we (helicopters) were limited to flying low level (usually below 150 feet above the ground – "agl") in order to allow separation between us and NATO fast jets patrolling the skies above us. Dodging under power wires suspended from pylons was an everyday occurrence; I remember creeping under telephone wires on the odd occasion! In those days the British Army of The Rhine (BAOR) lived in the field, on

---

[31] Close down their hatches and navigate and fight using simple glass periscopes – this was a significant degradation in tactical ability for them.

exercise, for approximately 8 months of the year. Looking after ourselves in all weathers became second nature, making the most of farm buildings to hide the helicopters around and then get a comfortable bed-space became second nature. As a Flight Commander I had carried out recces and knew exactly where I and my soldiers were likely to die should the Russians decide to cross the Iron Curtain.

*Figure 17 - Lynx Mk7 Anti-Tank Flight from my Gazelle.*

It was to some I guess a weird feeling, but not one any of us dwelt upon – it was just life. Talking of life, I also made the most of opportunities for adventurous training, skiing in the winter and climbing mountains in the summer. I qualified as a Joint Services Mountain Expedition leader and Windsurfing instructor, so thereafter managed at least 2 weeks away from work each year leading expeditions or adventurous training exercises for nearly the whole of the rest of my career. I heard that CSgt Bradshaw (my Sandhurst mentor) had re-joined his Battalion in Paderborn having finished his tour mentoring young officers at Sandhurst and flew down to their barracks to go and say hello. He loved this, and I was really pleased to be able to tell him he had been right to persuade me to stay during those early challenging weeks in Camberley. I was also able to take a Gazelle back to England for depth servicing and drop in to see my parents on route. As an ex-RAF Volunteer Reserves pilot my dad was chuffed to bits, and a few of the locals I was at school with came to have a quick look around the helicopter. Being on exercise with the AAC was slightly more civilised than with the infantry. We had to comply with the same fitness standards, carry out the same training in our NBC kit and live in the field just the same. However, we didn't have to live in trenches, but we did dig shell scrapes as some defence against an artillery strike, but as the helicopters were a little too big to dig into the ground, we used farm buildings and woods as "hides" camouflaging the helicopters with netting and blade camouflage sheets. Our armoured vehicle recognition skills were pushed to another level entirely; we had to be able to recognise every possible variation of all soviet armoured vehicles consistently having seen a photograph of a small part of the vehicle. This was so that a fleeting glimpse of an advancing enemy vehicle through the Gazelle overhead sight could be reported accurately, and by knowing the vehicles expected in a formation it was possible to advise where the soviet advance guard and main body of any offensive armoured column would be simply by recognising a specialist vehicle immediately. However, it wasn't all work, the Möhnesee (one of the reservoirs bombed by the Dam Busters 617 Squadron RAF during WW2) was only 5 miles away from the airfield and barracks. There was a very active sailing and windsurfing club there which I used most weekends. Skiing was available in the winter about an hour's drive away at Willingen, and there was a very active orienteering club at Soest – a sport I enjoyed immensely and was good enough to do reasonably well in – I wasn't the fastest runner by a long way, but my map-reading and appreciation of the realities of the ground as shown on the map was first class. There was a brilliant annual fair at Söest too, known as the "kermis"; a number of travelling fairs met there annually and set up their rides within the town streets: it was possible on many rides to reach out and almost touch the buildings swinging or whizzing past – very exciting, and the Germans always did beer and street food exceptionally well.

*Figure 18 - My end of tour present!*

# Chapter 10.

# Army Aviation Centre Middle Wallop & the 1ˢᵗ Gulf War.

After Germany I was posted back to the home of the AAC at Middle Wallop as Chief Signals Instructor at the School of Army Aviation. Before starting at Middle Wallop, I passed my 8 week Regimental Signals Officer course as top student at the Royal Armoured Corps Signals School, home of the Armoured Corps, Bovington, which didn't go down too well with the "tankies" as we called the Royal Armoured Corps. I then took control of a small team of very bright and lively AAC soldiers charged with ensuring the AAC could communicate effectively in all theatres of war. This was a really fun posting, albeit mostly away from tactical flying, where I learnt stuff which really helped me later in my career both as a Squadron Commander in the mountainous areas of Bosnia and before that in the deserts of Kuwait and Iraq. Luckily for me I managed to remain "current & competent" flying the Gazelle in support of ground training wing which is where AAC soldiers were taught to marshal, refuel and sling loads under helicopters, with the occasional longer VIP flight around the country thrown in for good measure. It was 1991 and the Iraq War had just blown up – Saddam driving his tanks into Kuwait in order to take control of the supply of oil to the rest of the world. One of the Germany based AAC units, 4 Regiment AAC based in Detmold were warned off to go as part of the NATO rescue effort. Back at Middle Wallop I immediately applied to be a BCR (Battle Casualty Replacement) as Gazelle pilots with my experience would be in high demand should the fighting be prolonged. At the same time, I applied for a post as a UNIKOM (United Nations Iraq Kuwait Mission) officer as I heard that it had been decided that when the war was won a peace-keeping force would be needed in the region. However, I was very disappointed to be told I wasn't being considered as a BCR as my post at Middle Wallop was "too important to gap"; only to be told about a week later that I was to go and train as a UNIKOM officer!

After literally another week had passed we deployed after a very hurried 3 days training – the war had finished the day before and we arrived in Kuwait by C130 to a day as dark as most nights – the fires burning where Saddam's forces had blown up the oil wellheads in Southern Iraq around the Bubiyan Island and Al Bahra Oilfields south of Um Qasr produced masses and masses of black smoke effectively making some areas of the desert sunless for weeks. I left my girlfriend in a house with no boiler, no hot water and lots of floorboards unfitted – I had been half-way through converting the house from oil fired air blown heating to a gas fired central heating system. Luckily it was the summer, so she got by using a kettle to heat water for washing, and we still had an electric shower over the bath! We married when I returned 6 months later – we stayed married for 25 years, but the strain of living with PTSD and her inability to understand it or talk about it (along with a few other major reasons I won't go into) eventually put an end to that as well in 2018. Living and working in the desert where a war had been fought, visiting Bedouin trading fairs where all manner of guns were being sold illegally, and eating MREs – the absolutely disgusting American version of our ration packs for 6 months was an amazing experience. I lived in a trench with a Russian Spetznas officer at one stage and woke up on my camp cot a few times to see stars above me "go out" for a few seconds whilst a camel spider[32] crawled along the outside of my mosquito net trying to get to the warm flesh beneath – absolutely petrifying! Visiting Omani and Egyptian infantry and armoured units stationed around the Iraq/Kuwait border was a highlight – such magnificent hosts and

---

[32] Camel spiders are up to 15cm across, exceedingly ugly but not usually poisonous, but they were thought to feed on camel flesh whilst the animal was alive – hence the name. The theory was that they injected an anaesthetic so that they could munch away undetected!

the friendliest Arabs I ever met. One of the unfortunate parts of the job in the early days of the tour was to find and deal with remains of any Iraqi forces who had perished in battle. There were a significant number of destroyed T55 and T62 battle tanks and MTLB troop carriers around the border region; the MTLB in particular had a penchant for bursting into flames when hit due to both rear doors being fuel tanks; very few soldiers escaped from them if the vehicle was hit. Although I didn't know any of these unfortunate souls, the number of grotesque corpses we came across no doubt added a little to the growing backlog of points towards a PTSD result in later life. One event which should have been a highlight was being asked to "re-capture" a Kuwait national's motor yacht which had been moved to Um Qasr when it was "liberated" by Iraqi forces during their occupation of Kuwait City. Having got a lift to Um Qasr we located the yacht and "stole" it one night, sailing at night down the river and out into the Gulf past "The Bridge Port of Mubarak the Great" and then past Shumaymah before turning left and mooring in Shuwaikh Port. The owner came to meet us and expecting at least a rolex or a gold ingot we were annoyed to be given a bottle of whisky each. The yacht must have been worth at least £1 million! I was very lucky to be able to fly here during my tour; because I had previously been charged with looking after a Chilean Air Force major whilst serving at Middle Wallop during what was called the Middle Wallop International Air Show whilst I was on my pilot's course. During that event military aircraft came from all over the World and the foreign visitors were allocated a young AAC officer to show them around. When I'd been in Kuwait for around 3 weeks, we heard that the Chilean Air Force were going to deploy 6 Huey H1H Iroquois helicopters under UN colours to provide a casevac service to the troops involved in the UNIKOM mission. I was tasked with designing SOPs for the CASEVAC system and went to meet the crews on their arrival to brief them. I was amazed to find their officer commanding was the very same officer I had looked after a few years before, and he insisted I come flying whenever I wanted to. Normally one would have to undertake a long conversion course to fly a different helicopter, but the Huey H1H[33] flew in a very similar way to the Gazelle, and it always had 2 pilots – so I was able to get a number of hours of Huey flying under my belt. Apart from needing to be aware of the "Huey Tuck" – a very dangerous flight phenomenon whereby increasing power too quickly whilst pushing the nose forward too aggressively when speeding up from the hover could result in the pilot finding it impossible to pull the nose back up (due to high pressure building up over the cabin roof) and the aircraft would "tuck" its nose further and further down until the blades impacted the ground, it was a relatively benign helicopter to fly, being powerful and smooth. One thing I did try was the famous engine off "spot turn", this was where sitting in a hover, the engine is shut down (switched off) and then the helicopter turned a full 360° whilst using the collective lever to keep it off the ground. The main rotor in a helicopter usually slows down quite quickly when pulling in pitch on the collective to cushion the landing whilst the blades are in free spinning mode – just as they are in autorotation, but the 2 blade Huey had massive blades and their inertia was legendary – there was enough to perform the spot turn manoeuvre and still be able to cushion the landing. I did it easily! Flying over the Iraqi desert in the Vietnam Vintage Huey H1H occasionally was a real treat. Although much bigger than the Gazelle I was used to, they handled in a very similar manner and had great visibility for a utility helicopter. We always flew with the doors off due to the extreme heat in the summer and as I always

---

[33] The Chilean Huey H1H were in fact some of those not thrown off the back of aircraft carriers by the US Navy after the Vietnam war and were sold to Chile sometime later by the USA. They had seen flight time in Vietnam in action!

flew with a Chilean pilot I never had to be in charge – I just got the exciting bit flying (or "poling") the aircraft at low level across the seemingly endless desert and wadis. We didn't have GPS, so the aircraft commander was responsible for keeping track of where we were using dead reckoning and a very few known landmarks – impressive stuff to watch and a lesson I learnt which made subsequent flying on the featureless prairies of Canada easy. I managed to amass around 100 hours flying the Huey – a quite unusual entry in my logbook as the AAC hadn't bought any Bell 212 helicopters, successors to the H series, at that stage. At the end of my tour, I flew back to Middle Wallop after just over 4 ½ months away – an amazing experience and one I'll never forget.

# Chapter 11.

# *9* Regiment Army Air Corps – Yorkshire.

Later, after my tour at Middle Wallop finished, I served back in Yorkshire with 9 Regiment AAC as the Regiment's senior Captain, the Adjutant. I was involved with the aftermath of a fatal Lynx accident on the 1$^{st}$ August 1989 where 3 young Junior Leaders were killed – trying to help the families come to terms with what had happened. There were nine servicemen on board. The pilot, Sergeant Paul Bennett AAC serving with 657 Squadron of the Army Air Corps, based at Oakington, Cambridgeshire was killed and sadly, three members of the Junior Leaders' Regiment, Royal Engineers, based at Old Park Barracks, Dover, Kent also died in the tragic accident. As Adjutant I flew occasionally – enough to remain competent and spent a considerable period on exercise as we built up the Regiment from 2 people (the CO and myself) to a fully formed airmobile aviation unit complete with 3 flying squadrons, its own air defence troop and infantry company. Before being allowed to get out alone in the Gazelle and fly people around the country I flew the normal annual check ride with one of the Regimental qualified helicopter instructors (QHIs). Major Bloo Anderson (the Regimental head-shed helicopter flying instructor or RQHI) decided to treat me to a bit of a test. Whilst flying around at approximately 4000' above the Yorkshire Gliding Club (where I originally learnt to fly and which was only a few miles from our Topcliffe Airfield base), he did the classic "what's that"? question so I looked out to the right and then he shut the engine down. He didn't retard the throttle which was a technique instructors used to let you practice an engine off landing at a known airfield location, he actually shut the engine down. No noise, no power, no spinning rotors and a nasty hole in the ground below us unless I bottomed the collective lever within half a second and then autorotated down to find a suitable field to land in. Having bottomed the collective I looked across the cockpit and I clearly remember him grinning at me and he said, *"what are you going to do now?"*. I replied, *"I'm going to restart the bloody engine and recover from autorotation!"* I knew I needed around 2,500' of clear airspace below us to be able to re-start the engine, bring it back up to power then re-engage the collective clutch (which allowed the rotors to keep spinning during autorotation even if the engine stopped) to provide power and torque to the main and tail rotors and allow us to climb away safely. I had one shot at this procedure, or we would be doing an autorotation landing for real into a farmer's field (or more probably the Yorkshire gliding Club cliff top site) rapidly approaching from below. I set the gazelle up for this engine off field landing as I rapidly went through the engine restart procedure and of course we got it all together in time to not have to land unannounced at the gliding club below us.

*Figure 19 - Airmobile Aviation Battlegroup Lynx Mk7 TOW.*

I passed my annual check ride with flying colours – and another "above the average grading"! I was also treated to a set of practice engine off landings at night – a very sporting evolution, but luckily this wasn't part of my annual check ride!

Later on, I earned an accolade from my CO as an extremely robust officer after one particularly wet and cold Winter exercise in Northern England where I and all my kit got absolutely soaked through and stayed that way for 2 weeks. I think physical robustness was never a problem for me – it is a simple state of mind to control the effects of being cold and wet, hungry or too hot and thirsty, but the mental side of being robust may have had a detrimental effect on coping with having seen so much death in my life so far. I'll never know if that is the case, but not complaining about anything, and being in a culture where it wasn't the done thing to discuss difficult incidents definitely played a part in my affliction boiling over around 20 years later. I reached 1000 hours rotary wing flying time on 2$^{nd}$ November 1990 whilst flying General Mike Rose from Chelsea Barracks in central London to Salisbury Plain Training Area (SPTA) for a troop visit then to York (HQ 2 Division). General Mike sat in the left hand front seat, and between us we managed to lose my 1/250,000 aeronautical chart which was sucked out of the window between SPTA and York, but luckily having done the route before and with a little help from the Lower Airspace Radar service boys and girls along the way we got to York, where having been born there and grown up locally I found the barracks without any problem!

Having passed my staff selection exam with flying colours during my deployment to Kuwait I was very surprised to be told that I was not selected to attend Staff College after my adjutant's tour. The support of a couple of full colonels at Middle wallop however was enough to ensure I was selected to go to Military College Shrivenham near Oxford and study for a master's degree in Guided Weapon Systems. I spent a very full-on year studying there from January to December 1993 working my butt off – 08:30 until

23:00 five days a week, and most of Saturday. That all paid off when I was awarded my master's degree in December 1993. Immediately we were awarded our degrees, we were then to be told where we were going to be posted next. I expected to be put in a staff job, hopefully something to do with guided weapons but was extremely excited to be told that I had been put forwards to the AAC Squadron Command Board and had been selected to head up an anti-tank squadron; 661 Squadron AAC based in Germany. In those days that meant flying Lynx and Gazelle helicopters so I knew immediately I would have to return to Middle Wallop to undertake a Gazelle refresher course and a Lynx conversion course. But, prior to that I would have to go to Warminster to undertake the All-Arms Squadron Commander Course, an 8-week classroom and field-based training evolution during January & February 1994. On this course we all played the part of unit commanders and sometimes lower-level positions on various exercise scenarios across SPTA. It was great fun, and we learnt a lot about how the Army operated in Battlegroup sized formations, with recce, armour (tanks), infantry, engineers, artillery and AAC all working together to achieve the mission, charging across the plain in armoured vehicles and attacking manned and realistic defensive positions, according to Soviet doctrine, both from armour and as infantry on foot or armour bourne or as recce forces. After that I headed back to Middle Wallop for a week's leave before starting my Lynx conversion.

# Chapter 12.

**Gazelle Refresher and Lynx Conversion Course at Middle Wallop.** Getting back into the Gazelle was easy, and I really enjoyed the course, 3 weeks of not too much pressure, basically re-learning how to throw the aircraft around at low level without breaking anything, and without crashing either. After that though came some trepidation – the Lynx was a very powerful twin engine helicopter (it had set the world record helicopter speed during level flight), and it had quite a complicated technical system with one major component (the gearbox) that was easy to break if the correct procedure wasn't followed exactly during the process of getting both engines to power the rotor blades. It was also a lot heavier, and quite a bit bigger with significantly less visibility out for the 2 pilots, so working in confined areas and tactical flying was much more involved. Crew co-operation was a major thing, and a big change from flying the Gazelle, a big proportion of which I had done solo or without another pilot in the 2$^{nd}$ front seat. I had learnt a lesson during my Army Pilot's Course, that preparation was key to survival on any fast-paced flying course in the Army; so, I spent a week of my pre-course leave sitting quietly in the Lynx hangar going over and over the 100 odd motions needed to get a Lynx up and running ready for flight from closed-down and switched off. I set the tone with the instructors during my first sortie when mine asked if I'd like to run through the engine start procedure following commands from my instructor. I turned and looked across the cockpit and with a cheeky grin said, *"I'd like to give it a go without prompts if I could Staff"*. SSgt Surtees grinned back at me and said, *"Are you sure Sir - it's pretty mind-boggling compared with the single engine Gazelle we have both flown previously?"*; I gulped and said *"yes, but I'd like to try the whole sequence"*. SSgt Surtees was by now thinking "OMG, Major Spink must think he's a bloody whiz kid" but gamely said *"Sure – go ahead – I'll stop you if you are going to break anything!"*. Five long minutes later his jaw was on the floor – the Lynx was running ready to lift, without a single prompt. That was a GOOD way to start an army flying course, which passed seamlessly from that moment on.

My second to last flight at Middle Wallop before passing my Lynx conversion course was as part of the infamous massed fly-on or as we used to call it "massed crash". During my time on the pilot's course there had been an International Airshow which included almost all the Gazelles, Scouts and Lynx in the AAC being brought back to the UK to take part in a massed semi-tactical fly forwards towards the spectators. In reality, what happened was that the Gazelles, Scouts and Lynx flew a low-level route out of sight of the members of the public attending a large open day at Middle Wallop, getting into position in 2 long lines approximately 2 miles away from the airfield. On a radio signal they would all rise up from their hidden positions to sit where they could see the audience through their sights, but the audience couldn't see them, or most of them at least. On another signal all would rise up a little more so that the fuselages were in direct line of sight, and then switch on their landing lights, surprising the audience with the near 130 helicopters all sitting in 2 lines approximately 2 miles away. To finish off the lines of helicopters would then fly forwards until they crossed the airfield boundary and then splitting in the middle, turn left or right and fly along the front of the crowd line giving everyone a fabulous view of all the helicopters whilst being bombarded by the noise and smell of avtur fuel. Fantastic! At the time I was on my Lynx conversion the higher-ups decided that we should do something equally as spectacular for the upcoming AAC Guidon parade. HRH the Prince of Wales (now of course King Charles) was going to present a new Guidon marked with latest AAC battle honours to our Colonel Commandant General Simon St John Little, and it was decided that instead of marching onto parade the parading AAC troops who were brought back from all AAC units worldwide for the occasion would be flown onto parade in as many Lynx as could be mustered.

*Figure 25 – My Lynx Conversion pre-Final Check Ride flight - no pressure!*

Luckily for me there was one Lynx left at Middle wallop which didn't have a right-hand seat crew allocated and it was decided that I would fly one of the Lynx commanded by an instructor onto and off the parade. We flew a long circuit picking up 6 troopers at a time, depositing them in formation in front of the now King Charles III. It was fabulous flying, and not very easy as the turbulence from around 25 heavy Lynx flying in close formation is formidable.

The next day, whilst most pilots were clearing up the mess left all over the airfield, and at the end of the conversion course having already "blued" my instrument flying training sorties gaining a Master Green Endorsement to my instrument licence, I flew my Final Handling Check with the head of Army Aviation Standards and managed another "Above the Average[34]" grading for that check ride too – a very happy squadron commander to be!

---

[34] During any flight check by an Army (or RAF/RN) qualified helicopter instructor a pilot being tested was awarded a grade which was recorded in his/her flying logbook and training record held by Aviation Standards Branch at Middle Wallop. The worst acceptable grading was "below average", with grades progressing through "average", "high average" and occasionally (for an officer at least) "above-the-average". Soldiers, as professional pilots who spent their whole career flying once trained usually attained "high average" or "above the average". Officers, who bounced between flying and staff appointments often attained "average" to "high average" gradings. During my career spanning over 2,000 hours of helicopter command time, we were generally tested twice a year and at the end of every flying course, I was lucky enough to receive one "high average" grading and the remainder were all "above-the-average".

# Chapter 13.

**Officer Commanding 661 Sqn AAC Gutersloh, Germany**. So, at the beginning of June 1994 I found myself back in northern Germany, Gutersloh this time, commanding 661 Squadron AAC with 6 Gazelle and 6 Lynx helicopters, with approximately 90 AAC soldiers and 30 REME under my charge. This was in most ways the perfect tour – Squadron command is the best time in any officer's life as it is your "ship to command" albeit usually with a HQ sitting directly above you. The role of a squadron commander was to fly, to get to know and lead my men and women and use the 12 aircraft under my command effectively in whatever scenario and environment we found ourselves. We worked hard and played hard too, and were a particularly close-knit bunch of officers, soldiers and wives. I was flying almost daily, splitting my flying time between Gazelle and Lynx and enjoying both. During a liaison trip back to England I was able to fly a Gazelle back to Easingwold to see my parents. Unfortunately, their garden was just too small to land on, but the local cricket pitch at the end of their drive was perfectly okay! At one stage all 3 Squadrons in the Regiment (1 AAC) were deployed into the field supporting Divisional training and based around the Mendig area in central Western Germany. The 3 flying squadron commanders, of which I was one, were in fierce competition to be selected to take their squadron to Bosnia to replace 664 Squadron, which belonged to one of the UK AAC regiments, in independent support of the UK Brigade deployed in a peacekeeping role in the Balkans theatre.

I had been pushing the blokes and women hard. I had just been on a task to Divisional HQ where I had seen 2 other Lynx which had just dropped off the Divisional Commander and his core team. All 3 Lynx had sat with rotors almost touching in the small landing site adjacent to the HQ, the crews chatting and having a laugh on the inter-aircraft radios for around 5 minutes whilst our various passengers deplaned and went off on their duties. One of the Lynx was from my squadron (SSgt "Radders" Radbourne), and it and the other (from 651 squadron) were going to lift and move to pick up a few more passengers from a field location before heading back to respective squadron locations to refuel men and aircraft. I was nearly out of fuel so was going to fly straight back to my Squadron location. Whilst making my final approach to land at my forward rearming & refueling point location, I thought I heard a faint "*mayday*" call in my flying helmet's headphones, immediately followed by a slightly garbled message from one of the Lynx which had been at the HQ a few minutes earlier concerning an accident. I didn't know which Lynx had been involved but losing one's men or women was something all Squadron commanders hoped would never happen during their tour as boss. Having very quickly landed and refueled, I took off for the reported location.

On arrival overhead I could clearly see one Lynx and its crew sitting in a field, but the other Lynx had obviously crashed nearby and was completely destroyed by fire. Parts of it were left in a trail I could see in a long line across the field in amongst the new arable crop. I landed and it was immediately apparent that the 651 Squadron Lynx had broken up in the air and that the crew, aircraft commander Sgt B and pilot Cpl B, had both been killed immediately. Sgt B, who I knew quite well, still sat in his cockpit seat where it had exited the aircraft during its break-up, he looked nearly normal – and was instantly recognisable, but was missing his left arm. Later on in my career, this seemingly minor factor may have become a defining trigger for my PTSD to begin to spin up during the latter part of my 2008/09 Afghanistan tour, and later on rage unchecked and out of control during a 2015 tour in Africa with Spanish Marines and the French Foreign Legion.

Having got out of the Lynx I walked up along the trail of damaged parts and remains of the Lynx until I came across one main rotor blade which had detached from the main rotor head and gearbox assembly, and then the rotor head itself – torn from the gearbox by the extreme forces involved when, obviously, one of the blades had detached from the set of 4, subjecting the aircraft to violent rotational vibration – tearing the aircraft apart in mid-air. The Lynx has a titanium rotor head which is extremely rigid, and so utilises a tie-bar method of attaching the rotor blades which allows movement of each blade in pitch whilst whirling around above the helicopter, but also holding the blades tightly to the main rotor head and gearbox assembly so changing the direction the helicopter flies in. As an engineer it was immediately clear to me that a tie-bar, in effect a long wire wound round and round 2 bobbins and sealed in a sort of polyurethane sheath to prevent corrosion, had come apart – something that should never have been possible. Having reported this fact back to HQ I was tasked to lead the site preservation effort[35] and I gathered my Squadron around me at the crash site and we sifted carefully through the site marking all the bits and especially flagging anything we thought might provide for evidence for the ensuing investigation. We also guarded our comrade's bodies where their remains lay for the next couple of days whilst the accident investigation team from the UK arrived,

---

[35] Later in my career I was qualified at Cranwell University as an aircraft accident investigator. My experience on the Mendig site helped enormously during the course. For any military aircraft accident, it is vital to preserve the site of the accident until the investigation team can be assembled and flown out. They needed to ascertain whether or not there was a likelihood of further accidents if the cause had been a technical failure. In this case the whole Lynx fleet was grounded before the investigators arrived due to my testimony at the scene of the accident – the main rotor tie-bar should never be able to fail if manufactured properly.

and the accident site was investigated. Again, apart from rigorous questioning by the accident investigation team, there was no form of post experience de-brief, so any survivor guilt feelings were simply suppressed and eventually allowed to fester. Worse was to come.

During the next few months Westland helicopters, who designed and built the Lynx, worked out that the material waterproofing the wires which made up the "tie-bars" was defective and that the wires had become contaminated and then corroded leading to their eventual demise - which had allowed a blade to depart the rotor head in flight – destroying the aircraft through the enormous rotational vibration set up by the imbalanced rotor head. The complete Lynx fleet was grounded, a really unusual event, and all tie bars removed for testing. Some weeks later The CO and I flew the first Lynx to be cleared for flight with old but checked tie-bars – we were both waiting for the bang throughout the flight, which luckily never happened – but it had to be done to show the Regiment's pilots and groundcrew that it was safe to fly Lynx again. The technical checks did their job, no other Lynx tie bar gave way throughout the remaining 20 odd years of flying before the Wildcat helicopter took over their role, and the Lynx were all retired.

My calm method of coping with the enormous stress caused by that event marked me out for my CO, and the fact that my squadron aircraft were the only ones to subsequently make a field rendezvous with him during some pretty atrocious weather for an Orders group in mid Germany on a following exercise sealed my fate. During a subsequent weekly "orders" meeting back at Gutersloh, whilst I was absent en-route to the UK for a holiday, the CO informed the other 2 squadron commanders that I had been chosen to take my squadron to Bosnia to replace 664 Squadron at the end of their 6-month stint in a few months' time.

The Adjutant (the senior captain assistant to the CO) caught up with me whilst I was on a ferry from Vlissingen to Harwich and gave me the good news. I was ecstatic – a command appointment on operations with no-one in the in-theatre aviation command chain above me was nirvana for any army aviation officer.

I devised and was authorised to conduct a 3-month package of intensive training, for my squadron aircrew and groundcrew alike. This including deck landing training in the UK at Portland when HRH (as he was then) Prince Andrew was senior pilot and was incredibly helpful towards us, getting out of bed at an ungodly hour to greet me and show us our accommodation following a 7-hour delay in arrival due to having to wait for severe fog to clear in Belgium.

I also flew 2 Lynx up to Woodcote House school, where the boys were able to climb aboard and ask us all about the Lynx, its weapons and upcoming roles in Bosnia. During annual TOW missile firing practice at Otterburn ranges I fired 3 missiles at tank hulk targets some 4 kilometers from my Lynx, seeing 2 hit their targets but also having one go "rogue", a reasonably common occurrence as the missiles we used we at the end of their stock life. The missile climbed almost straight up and back over my head as I cut the command wire which would cause it to crash within the range area, hopefully missing myself and my other Lynx. Not forgetting the ground and engineering elements of my Squadron we completed NBC and first aid training, and a full weapons range package which I personally designed to put my guys through as realistic set of training and scenarios as possible at the NITAT facility in Sennelager. Realistic, challenging and noisy with more ammunition to expend in one week-long package than the Squadron had seen across the whole last 3 years, they and I loved it.

*Figure 20 - My Lynx in the UK during Pre-Bosnia Training.*

We had converted onto NVG during my Lynx conversion course and had been steadily gaining hours of experience flying tactically in known and pre-recced areas as a single ship formation. However, Cat 2 NVG flying had been cleared by HQ Land (Aviation) and so we started learning how to fly long routes at extremely low level, using the ground tactically just as we would in daylight as single ships; and then we moved onto Cat 3 flying – the difference here being that we flew multiple Lynx in close formation just as we did during daylight tactical sorties. My squadron was the only one in the Regiment capable of Cat 3 NVG flying, through the amount of experience and competency that we had strived to attain and maintain, and we pushed hard to get as much of this challenging flying as possible under our belts. It was exceptionally exciting to be able to manoeuvre between 3 and 6 Lynx all in close formation into fire positions after routing to the location at low level, all on NVG. The green and ghostly images were sometimes hard to decipher when the starlight levels were low, but nap of the earth flying and particularly wire crossing drills on NVG certainly made us pay maximum attention.

In final preparation for our deployment, we finished up our training by completing lots of night vision goggle flying routes in the mountains of Wales including flying the "mach-loop" at around 50' agl and then packed up and flew back home to Gutersloh. We then had a couple of weeks' leave and subsequently shipped out in 2 C130 RAF transport planes. My daughter Hebe managed to walk her first steps during my last pre-deployment meeting with my second in Command, Captain Alan Gray – luckily the meeting was in my dining room, he noticed and stopped me mid-brief so I could witness it for myself. I nearly forgot to mention, my son Hugo joined his sister Hebe 3 days before we shipped out – I wasn't to see him again for over 5 and a half months, nor return home properly for nearly 9.

# Chapter 14.

***B***osnia – 2 Tours in One. On 2$^{nd}$ August 1995, my Squadron (661 Squadron Army Air Corps) arrived in Split, Croatia where a RN Seaking Flight was based under Lt Cdr DD Royal Navy, and I flew with a senior pilot from the outgoing AAC squadron from Split via Mostar (where the famous arched stone bridge had been destroyed) into Bosnia and up to my future home at Gornji Vakuf. After 2 more recces in country with the departing squadron's QHI (one flown in daylight and one at night on NVG), I took over the role of providing the Lynx squadron for Op GRAPPLE, the UNPROFOR (United Nations Protection Force) mission in central Bosnia – a war torn country with shelling taking place regularly 5 miles to our Northwest. Our overarching mission given to me on 5 August 1995 was to assist in maintaining a fragile peace between the mainly muslim Bosnians and orthodox Serbian forces. We had a very busy and exciting tour with the UN, albeit the landscape was destroyed, and many civilians murdered during the UN's time in Bosnia.

The whole in-country part of the operation was run from an HQ in an old factory at Gornji Vakuf in central Bosna Herzegovina by a UK brigadier and his HQ staff, supported by a logistics base at Split in Croatia. On my first day in Gornji Vakuf I went into the HQ to have a chat with the Brigadier and some of his staff to get an updated picture of what our missions were likely to be. Walking up the stairs I was amazed to see someone I knew, but obviously he was not in the Army as he was very overweight and wearing very scruffy civilian clothes. He had been my boss on one of the Shell ships and had been a bit of an aggressive twat to say the least. He was now a low-grade civil servant charged with keeping the armoured vehicle and aviation fuel stocks up to date. The look on his face when he realised that I was now commanding the squadron of helicopters he was responsible for providing fuel for, and way outranked him was brilliant. Karma!

As the only helicopters allowed to operate in the country were the white painted UN helicopters; 661 Squadron AAC (which I commanded) and a small Norwegian helicopter detachment (consisting of 2 Bell 212 helicopters) based in Tusla some 120km distance to our North-North-West, were exceedingly busy. We started our tour operating out of a cramped factory yard, with high lighting poles around all sides and living in tents – not a very safe location as none of the lights worked and the risk of clipping a rotor on one during landing or take-off being very high; so I decided to build a full helicopter operating site from nothing, begging for some unused container type accommodation buildings which I'd seen stored at Split to be shipped up to Gornji Vakuf on army vehicles, then putting them together ourselves. We also built 8 helicopter landing pads with the help of the Royal Engineers field troop, 2 big enough for Seaking or Chinook, and based 4 of my Lynx there. Adding a working fireplace and shower / loo bock with accommodation for the whole detachment where the OC (me) surprised all his men by proving himself an excellent welder – a skill learnt whilst working for Shell, we made a safe and relatively comfortable operating base. Our tasks included moving politicians and high-ranking military visitors around the country, gathering the commanders of various warring factions together for peace accord meetings, providing top cover for UN convoys and for visits to warlords by politicians and top brass, as well as planning offensive operations should they be needed.

One such offensive operation was to fly at night on goggles to a place called Maglaj approximately half-way to Tuzla where a Serbian battle tank had been converted to run out of a mine entrance on rail tracks laid high up a mountainside mine entrance overlooking the town. The tank was rolled out occasionally and fired shells down into the town, where a British army unit was housed – injuring some British troopers. The operation called for one of my Lynx to take the tank out (we thought it was a modified T55) using our thermal imaging roof sight and FITOW (Further Improved Tube-launched Optically tracked Wire-guided) Anti-Tank Guided Weapon (ATGW)) missile system. That would have been the first engagement by a UK helicopter outside the Gulf War, but although we planned the mission and flew a reconnaissance covertly at night on NVG, we were never tasked to go.

*Figure 21 - My Lynx near Gornji Vakuf.*

Another mission I planned but which was never undertaken was to lead a UK Battlegroup advance into Sarajevo at night, flying our Lynx tactically at extremely low level on NVG as a FITOW equipped vanguard force, obliterating any armoured vehicles the Serbs put in our way.

On 12th August I flew Brigadier P up onto Mount Igman

overlooking Sarajevo, and he had wandered off to talk to the troops.  Sitting in the cockpit I had just started my Lynx's engines having seen him starting to walk back the 200m to the helicopter when I heard, *"Charlie-Charlie-One[36] rounds incoming, repeat rounds incoming, out"* over the tactical radio used by the mountain top observation post Brigadier P was visiting.  Christ – somewhere on the mountain where my Lynx and a RN Seaking were sitting, artillery rounds fired from the outskirts of Sarajevo were likely to be landing any second.  Brigadier P was still over 100m away from the aircraft and out of comms; he had no idea artillery rounds would be landing probably any second now.  Dispatching my door gunner to run out, he grabbed the Brigadier whilst I got the Lynx's twin engines driving the rotors up to flying speed, and then with the Seaking in tow a few seconds later we lifted and exited the area very rapidly.  Artillery rounds landed around the very area we had been sitting approximately 30 seconds later – that was an exceedingly close call!

Two of my pilots, Sgt Dean Attridge (AAC) and Lt Andy R (RN) managed to achieve their respective 1,000 hours flying time together on a night sortie.  A bottle of champagne welcomed them on their return to Gornji Vakuf.  The mountains in Bosnia ranged from around 2,000' to just over 8,000' above sea level.  Gornji Vakuf was situated at approximately 4,000' and surrounded by 8,000' mountains.  On 17th September I suffered an engine failure whilst climbing up Route Diamond, one of the gravel Main Supply Routes winding along through mountain passes, which followed the valley leading NE from Gornji Vakuf and eventually to Sarajevo.  Seeing the port engine oil pressure warning light come

---

[36] *"Charlie-Charlie-One"* means all callsigns listening on that radio net.

on, just as the warning buzzer went off, I checked the oil pressure gauge to see it reading well into the red and rapidly heading towards zero. Cpl "Redders" Redman continued to fly the Lynx whilst I shut down the failing engine to stop it destroying itself and us with it, and then taking control just managed to turn the Lynx around in the steep sided very tight valley without hitting the trees. Continually descending as we had 6 passengers on board and not enough power on one engine to maintain height, I selected a landing site outside the cramped and dangerous helicopter landing site we operated from – a possible minefield, but the only flat piece of ground which we could safely make a single engine approach to. Redders got the "book" out and quickly made the calculations to work out our minimum safe flying speed and best run-on speed for landing; as there was not enough power to come into the hover. Luckily the landing which entailed skidding along the ground for a short distance increasing the chances of hitting a buried mine went smoothly, and after calling out a Royal Engineer team to check around us for mines we were able to climb safely out of the aircraft and walk back into the camp.

On another occasion very soon after arriving in theatre I was flying a Lynx up a steep valley above Gornji Vakuf with Lt Peter Cooper as my recently qualified pilot to go to Tomislavgrad Plain on a night training trip – mountain flying using night vision goggles. HQ Aviation UKLF had denied us permission to plan to land in bad weather using our knee mounted GPS satellite navigation sets, which was a very recent addition to the equipment carried on the Lynx. It hadn't been proven whether it was accurate enough or not, so we were supposed to continue to use the old inertia-based TANS navigation system in an emergency situation. I decided this was utter bollocks as the TANS was inherently unreliable and could tell us we were in one position whilst we could actually be up to a nautical mile or more away after a long flight, and so I designed then check-flew a GPS based approach into Gornji Vakuf from the north.  The only problem with doing this was that the flight path would take us through an area under infrequent but common artillery shelling – but as the same was true of using the TANS inertial system as an approach aid, I thought the risk worthwhile.  The technique was simply to fly a route waypoint to waypoint on the GPS ensuring that we didn't let down (descend) any further than heights which we knew to be clear of cumulo-granite (mountains) at each waypoint, gradually slowing down and descending to ground level by the last waypoint.  It worked perfectly in the clear blue sky of one of our first days based at Gornji Vakuf and hopefully none of my pilots would have to use it for real.  That night I was flying hands-on as the Lynx climbed slowly up the ever increasingly steep and high sided valley, and my NVG suddenly "closed down" producing absolutely no image of the mountain valley ahead of us.  I asked Peter if he was okay, and he reported that the same thing had happened to his goggles.  That meant it was unlikely my goggles were at fault and that something had happened outside to "close-down" their ability to show us the ghostly green picture of what was ahead of us.  Only 2 things would do that – flying into cloud or flying into heavy falling snow, neither of which would have been particularly visible in our goggles before we flew into them.  I immediately started an emergency maximum power climb, which meant bringing the nose up until the airspeed dropped to 40 knots, then levelling out and climbing with both engines straining at maximum power hoping that we would avoiding flying into the mountainside.  I remembered how difficult I had found instrument flying during my training at Middle Wallop and was so thankful for that 3$^{rd}$ instructor realising why I was having such a hard time of it.  Once we were settled in the climb I handed over to Peter, and whilst monitoring his flying and the instruments very closely selected the emergency radio frequency and called a "Pan Pan Pan" over the air to callsign "Magic" an AWACS aircraft constantly circling overhead Bosnia whose job was to control all fast jet traffic and execute a search for any downed aircraft crews, and informed them of my emergency climb which could put us into the path of any fast jets patrolling overhead. They immediately put an exclusion box for all other aircraft around us which "followed" us up the mountain side and into clear air above it. Continuing the emergency climb we heaved a sigh of relief as we passed 8,000 feet, still in cloud which was now starting to produce ice on the aircraft, but clear of the highest mountain in the area, so safe for now as the Lynx could cope with quite a considerable accumulation of ice before the added weight overcame the power needed to continue flight even at that altitude. I quickly worked out that we didn't have enough fuel to be able to fly to the coast and get a radar assisted approach into Split, and there was no-where else to go but back to Gornji Vakuf sitting smack bang in the middle of a steeply sided valley with mountains rising 4,000 feet at either side. After a nanosecond's thought I decided we would fly over Bugojno at 8,000 feet, clear of the mountains and then use the GPS procedure I'd designed a few weeks before to let down through the steeply sided valley right onto to our base at Gornji Vakuf.

We were possibly going to be flying through sky filled with artillery shells, but we wouldn't see them as it was 10/10ths cloud down to about 300' above our base. The "Big Sky theory" said aircraft were very unlikely to be hit by shells in flight, and if we didn't do something fast the ice build-up on the Lynx would cause us to crash, and the only other possibility was to run out of fuel – not clever! After a tense 20 minutes descending along my invisible line in the middle of the valley we popped out of the cloud with Gornji Vakuf headquarters' very welcome lights showing us the way home. My immediate action was to ensure all my crews had the GPS approach logged in their GPS both for Gornji Vakuf and for Tomislavgrad refueling site.

Later in the tour I flew Malcolm Rifkind from Gornji Vakuf over the mountains to Sarajevo to meet Lt Gen Rupert Smith on 18 September – taking incoming small arms fire (we could hear the "crack crack" as it passed close to us) as I was in-bound to Sarajevo airport but without sustaining any hits. I knew General Rupert well as he had been Brigade Commander at Soest in Germany during my first field army flying tour. We had a quick chat then he was off bounding across the airport towards cover with Malcolm Rifkind in tow. Renowned BBC reporter Kate Aide visited Gornji Vakuf and was flown in one of my Lynx whilst doing a report for BBC News and managed her usual trait of being a bullet magnet, but luckily the Lynx wasn't hit, its crew also hearing the "*crack*" "*crack*" as rounds passed close by but missed.

In December 1996 we were informed that we would stay beyond the normal end of tour and rotate to be under IFOR command – bedding in the arriving NATO Divisional units before returning home after some 9 months away. Apart from changing the colour of my Lynx from UN white back to camouflage green and grey under IFOR, the change wasn't that big for us. We fitted our TOW missile launchers to one side of the aircraft leaving the GPMG on its door mount on the other and carried a number of FITOW anti-tank missiles brandishing our door mounted GPMG more obviously when flying into areas controlled by the Serbs. A whole regiment of AAC helicopters, 3 Regiment AAC, deployed to Ploce on the Croatian coast, but they along with all other helicopters supporting IFOR were not allowed to fly across the border into Bosnia, and so my Squadron alone remained incredibly busy moving warring faction commanders and others around. We also set up a couple of aviation strike missions: one involving just 2 Lynx and one involving the whole squadron.

The latter, full Squadron mission, was an advance to contact in the vanguard of any IFOR advance into Sarajevo. It was probably going to be flown at night and so we practiced some of the very close quarter flying on NVG that we had been used to in Germany, armed with up to 8 FITOW missiles each. The flying was known as cat 3 NVG and involved flying at around 2 rotors diameter distance apart whilst also flying literally a few feet above the ground. The lead aircraft had to route around obstacles such as big trees and buildings in such a manner that allowed the remaining aircraft in the formation to miss them too. It involved an enormous amount of planning when training in Germany with recces being flown down the exact route. Here, potentially under fire we had out of date maps and no ability to fly the actual routes in preparation. It was a very risky evolution but would have presented any Serb aggressive force with an overwhelming barrage of anti-tank weapons fired from seemingly no-where at night had we been called upon to lead an advance into Sarajevo. Our task was to lead the IFOR ground troops into the edges of Sarajevo dealing with any Serb armoured vehicles as we moved forwards. It was exciting stuff but not needed as the Serbs stopped refusing to bow to IFOR demands and the mission was put back on the shelf.

The 2-ship mission was potentially very exciting, and we flew a reconnaissance of the sortie one night in pitch blackness, straining to see through our NVG. Our task was to destroy a Serb tank (probably a T55 but possibly a T60) which had been mounted on rails and hidden in a mountainside ore mine entrance. It was pushed out infrequently and used to shell a UK patrol base in the northern part of our AOR. The shelling or direct fire from the tank had injured a few British soldiers and so we were tasked to take the tank out with a FITOW missile the next time they emerged from the mine. We devised a route which meant creeping up around a shoulder of an adjacent mountain a few feet above the trees for around 8 kilometers, then sitting in the hover to acquire the mine entrance in the roof mounted TOW sight. We had approximately one hour duration planned which should have been long enough to watch and wait for the tank to appear. The recce went exceptionally well, with some very exciting flying in minimal light conditions for the NVG. The time of flight for the missile would have been around 20 seconds but unfortunately, the Serbs decided to not use the tank again – either that or it got stuck in the mine.

I had another bird strike, just like in the Gazelle in Northern Ireland, but this time the outer layer of the semi-armoured glass of the Lynx windscreen simply cracked on my side and we replaced it at the end of the sortie. I also had a slightly worrying sotie and then another which ended in an emergency as we neared the end of the tour. Following the rescue of Captain Scott O'Grady USMC following 6 days escaping and evading after his F16 was shot down by a 2K12 Kub anti-aircraft missile, the local mujahedeen had decided that they wanted to find a downed aircrewman and chop his/her head off on TV. Any aircrew would do. I was flying east of Sarajevo shortly after Scott was found when my radar warning receiver went off, warning me that I was being tracked by a 2S6 anti-aircraft missile system radar. The missiles were IR guided but initially steered towards the target by a ground-based radar, and one of these had just locked onto us. Dropping steeply down to almost ground level I put some cumulo-granite between us and the probable location of the 2S6 site and broke the radar lock. Calling "Magic" on VHF I told them what had happened and the bearing from my current position to the radar and got a laconic drawl back asking me to wait! A few minutes later on the secure frequency the "Magic" operator asked me if I would climb back up and see if the 2S6 locked onto me again. Jesus! Didn't he know we were a helicopter without ejection seats and would probably not survive a multiple 2S6 launch against us? I decided to climb up quickly and then roll off the top into a maximum angle of descent to expose the

Lynx for as short a time as possible and as I approached 3000' above ground level, got another lock signal from my radar warning receiver. Informing "Magic" of the bearing I was told to wait and 30 seconds later told to climb slightly and look back down the bearing. A big flash and plume of smoke showed me exactly where the 2S6 had just been immolated by a 500lb bomb. That, I guess, was payback for the F16.

A couple of days after this incident I had a hydraulic failure on my Lynx whilst close to Sarajevo, en route back to Gornji Vakuf. The problem with the Lynx is that although it has 2 hydraulic systems, they are not quite mutually redundant and the loss of one can lead to the loss of the other. Without hydraulics the Lynx is impossible to control, so the normal response to this emergency is to land and wait for the AA or RAC – no, I mean the REME, to come and mend it. But if we did that it was likely we would be spotted and possibly captured, so I elected to fly hands-on back to GV in the hover taxi with my pilots' eyes glued to the other hydraulic system's gauge. If that pressure began to fall he had to warn me and I would simply fly the Lynx onto the deck, wherever we were. I reckoned if that pressure began to fall I might have around 10 seconds to get the Lynx on the ground in one piece before it flew itself to the site of the subsequent crash! We made it back safely – probably the longest fast hover taxi in history.

We were lucky and all my Squadron returned safely from our 9-month long tour. Others weren't so lucky. A soldier walked into the spinning tail rotor of a Seaking on the pad at my Split base and unfortunately was killed immediately. 3 Regiment Army Air Corps which deployed as part of the IFOR NATO force and were based in Ploce on the Croatian coast, unable to legally fly in Bosnia–Herzegovina lost a Lynx into the sea alongside a small island off Ploce in deep water with 4 men killed. A Lynx from the following

Regiment (which replaced my Squadron at Gornji Vakuf) also lost a Lynx just outside the Gornji Vakuf forward operating base killing 2 aircrew and an engineer on board.  A week after the Ploce accident (with the reason for it still unknown) I had flown down the Mostar valley, past the destroyed bridge at Mostar, and past where I had picked up some of the evilest men involved in ethnic cleansing in order to help broker a peace agreement, to visit 3 Regiment AAC. We spent the day and night in their tented camp – a far cry from the portacabin accommodation we had built for ourselves at Gornji Vakuf - briefing the 3 Regiment command team[37] on operations in-country, advising on routes, danger areas, hazards and Serb tactics etcetera should they be allowed to enter the war-zone.  During the evening the Regiment put on an excellent in-the-field dinner night - the tables adorned with magnificent pieces of regimental "silver" (made from cardboard and silver paper) which are still used occasionally back in their Wattisham, Suffolk officer's mess, with food made up by the unit's amazing army chefs from army rations including steak & kidney "babies heads", and a few bottles of beer.  I collapsed into a camp bed requisitioned from the quartermaster just in time to get my legally required 8 hours sleep before heading off back to my main operating base at Split the next morning.

Approximately 20 minutes after taking off whilst transiting from Ploce towards Spilt I suffered a serious engine problem in my Lynx, over the sea with 3 crew and 6 passengers aboard.  The coastline was steep mountainous slopes straight down into the sea, with a very narrow road running along it, and the occasional rocky beach

---

[37] 3 Regiment AAC was led by Commanding Officer John Greenhalgh who had earned a DFC firing SS11 missiles at an Argentine gun position in the Falklands war.

but both far too narrow to land on with the Lynx's main rotor being just over 10m in diameter. The weather was dog-shit – sea haze and clouds down to approximately 400'agl which meant I could not climb up and over the coastal mountains, and so I briefed the passengers to open the doors, tighten straps and expect to crash land or ditch in the sea. I told them I would aim to ditch as close to the shore as possible so we wouldn't sink too far – but in places the water went straight down to well over 20m within a rotor span of the shoreline. If we did land in the sea, I knew we would turn upside down very quickly, and then sink like a stone to the bottom – probably a long way down. We would be very lucky if we all got out, especially my pilot and I sitting in heavily armoured seats and wearing bulky and heavy body armour to boot. I spent most of the whole remaining 18 minutes of the flight trying to identify which engine was misbehaving; something which is normally abundantly clear, making sure I knew what the ever changing minimum airspeed we needed to be able to fly level if one engine completely failed was so that I would instantly know whether we could "fly-away" if one engine failed or would immediately be forced onto on a downward trajectory and have to ditch, and working out what speed we needed to fly at to minimise the impact if we had a complete engine failure whilst over the sea or approaching over the short spit of land approaching the barracks at Split. For some of the flight we did not have the power with 6 passengers on board to maintain height if the engine failed – so I expected to have to make a running ditching into the sea. Spending 20 minutes over the sea with nowhere to land on if the engine problem became terminal was a very unsettling trip for all, even though apparently, as I found out after we had eventually landed, I was very calm throughout the emergency, and so therefore were the passengers. As I landed at Split one of the Lynx engines actually blew up sending a few 50p sized pieces of engine casing flying out of the back of the engine – a very close shave!

The rest of the tour went very well, Brigadier Richard Dannatt MC replaced Brigadier P as Brigade Commander and I got on very well with him. One day I flew him from Gornji Vakuf north up to Sipovo to visit some of his men. It had been snowing a lot, the first snow of the year and was also pretty foggy, just within our legal limits for flying. I managed to slip under a fog layer just as the mountain valley we were following turned downhill, skipping over some telephone wires still standing after such a long period of fighting, and after contouring down the valley for about 20 miles we saw the headquarters we needed to land at. Coming into a hover to have a look at the best route in through all the trees and telephone wires close to the HQ, Brigadier Richard said to drop him where we were in an area of paddock like fields as there were lots of trees and wires close up to the command complex; and so I sat in a hover[38] just above the snow. I had been there before the snow fell and settled and was thinking about the fact that I couldn't see any fences which I was sure I remembered were situated around the fields and was just about to warn Brigadier Richard when he launched himself out of the door. The snow must have been at least 6 feet thick (which was why the fences around the fields had disappeared) and he almost disappeared completely! We waited until he appeared above the surface of the snow field and white out caused by the rotor recirculation around 50m away, waved at us and then sauntered into the command complex as if nothing had happened. He was a superb boss, taking aviation advice whenever offered or needed and quickly acting on it.

---

[38] although we had skids on our Lynx, it being a Mk 7, we had not yet fitted the specialist snow landing skids, so I was wary of landing on the snow and subsequently sinking on one side – tilting enough to hit the blades on the snow or ground underneath, probably destroying the aircraft.

My QHI, SSgt Chris Hearn[39] and I flew a Lynx back to Split one day so that I could spend the evening with the half of my squadron and engineers who were operating from Croatia in support of my mission based out of Gornji Vakuf deep in Bosnia Herzegovina. I was hands on pilot for a change as Chris, who had thousands of hours experience, was my squadron instructor or QHI, and we were making the most of the otherwise slightly boring trip by practicing emergencies every now and again – good practice for me as I seemed to have more than my fair share of things going awry with my Lynx when I was flying them during my tour as Squadron Commander. We landed without issue at my base in Split (which is now where Trogir Marina sits) after going through the annoying procedure of first of all landing at Split airport to go and clear Croatian customs before starting up again and hopping over the road (almost) to land at my main base. Having shut down the rotors and engines we walked into my command post and got an update from my operations staff. In the background I heard a panicky call for help from an unknown British voice saying there had been a really bad road traffic accident on the main route down from Bosnia through the coastal mountains and into Split (which was also the main operating base for the logistics effort supporting all troops in Bosnia) and that 2 British soldiers were very badly injured just over the Bosnian border with Croatia and needed MEDEVAC immediately. I immediately told Chris to go and start the Lynx up and spent a few minutes trying to get an exact location from the very upset squaddie on the other end of the radio. The accident site was inside Bosnia which meant if we followed normal agreed practice we should fly into Spilt airport, shut down, walk into customs and then wait for Croatian border paperwork to be

---

[39] Chris was later commissioned, reaching Lt Col.

signed before we were allowed to take off and fly across the border and into Bosnia to the accident site! Meanwhile traffic on the radio suggested an ambulance was being dispatched but this would take at least 40 minutes to get to the casualty, and it sounded as though one of the soldiers was going to bleed out if we didn't get there quickly. I made a decision to lift and fly directly to the accident site which at maximum speed (the Lynx held the World speed record for helicopter flight) would take me around 7 minutes as I could fly in a straight line between base and accident site. Having taken off into the hover I called Split airport and requested departure direct to the casualty site, giving them details of exactly where that was and the likely injuries. Incredibly they refused, and insisted I hop over the airport and "custom-in" as usual before heading off legally into the country. I replied I wasn't going to do that and would depart immediately at very low level on a heading direct to the casualty keeping clear of any departing or arriving "traffic" flying into/out of Split airport. At that point someone else came on the Split radio and said that they would shoot me down if I did that! Bollocks, this British soldier was probably going to die, and I was pretty sure (having my master's degree in Guided Weapons safely in my back pocket) that the missile counter measures on the Lynx would spoof any missile in the Croatian inventory, so I asked Chris and my rear crewman if they were happy to take the risk with me – to which both immediately said yes. I transitioned into forward flight and told Split ATC that *"we were headed for the location of a serious accident site, and they could try and shoot me down if they wanted to"*! Of course, they didn't, and we got to the accident site in about 6 minutes. It was immediately clear what had happened – one gigantic main battle tank transporter had run down the mountain road into the back of another which had previously broken down. Unfortunately, the 2 soldiers working on the first truck hadn't seen or heard the run-away vehicle and had been crushed between both. There were no ambulances or other suitably qualified help within sight. I landed in the middle of the road completely blocking it and my air crewman ran the 50m to assist extracting the 2 injured soldiers from the wreckage. One of them had a leg hanging off and the other badly mangled, the other was badly crushed and in severe shock. Making a snap decision I decided to put the 2 injured soldiers into the back of the Lynx and fly them to a German Field Hospital located literally a kilometer up the coast from my base at Split. That meant crossing back into Croatia (again without customs clearance) and once again, the Croatians said they would shoot us down, but I ignored them – one of the 2 soldiers was going to die very soon if not treated immediately. My exceptionally talented and calm air crewman kept the pair alive in the back, putting in the first intravenous drip he had ever done for real, stemming the bleeding and keeping them both awake and alive. I radioed ahead to the field hospital, luckily not having to use my German as they spoke excellent English. Within seconds of landing both soldiers were whisked away by full A&E crews on stretchers, so we took off and returned to Split.

About an hour after landing, I got a phone call from a very irate Group Captain (2 ranks above me, but in the RAF) ranting and raving down the wire. He was in charge of the Split logistic base and was incandescent because I had caused a diplomatic incident with the Bosnian and Croatian authorities, and this might blot his copybook before he retired in a few years' time! I managed to bite my tongue – this "officer" had probably never been in combat and was obviously wetting himself at the thought of being told off by the RAF chain of command; I told him that I had done what was necessary to save lives and would brief my own Commanding officer – the Brigadier in Gornji Vakuf. His parting words were *"you haven't heard the back of this"*. Around 20 minutes later I got another call, this time from the senior German surgeon at the field hospital, a German Group Captain. He wanted to thank me and the crew for saving both soldiers' lives – one had lost a leg but the other would eventually be fully fit again. He told me that if they had waited for the paramedics and British ambulance, they would likely both have died, so job well done as far as he and I were concerned. I told him what the RAF Logistics Base commander had said to me during his rant and he said that he would personally go above his head and explain the situation with the theatre chain of command. A day later we flew back up to Gornji Vakuf, passing through customs as normal. On landing I went to speak to the British Commanding Officer Brigadier P and explained what had happened. His simple reply was "well done, I'll sort this", and that was the end of that. I later heard that the RAF officer had tried to get me sacked but had been told *"where to go"* by the Army chain of command and was short toured (returned home early) himself shortly afterwards.

We had a 2 ship Lynx flight from 657 Squadron attached to my Squadron for a while to bolster our numbers one of them flown by SSgt Fred M who had been one of my instructors on the advanced rotary phase of my middle wallop training, and we flew a few missions together. This included some very exciting flying providing armed aviation cover during some high-powered liaison meetings between Brigadier P and various Serbian leaders. SSgt Fred M also flew a very daring rescue mission accompanied by two of my pilots in a second Lynx to extract the crews of 2 scimitar reconnaissance vehicles which had strayed into a minefield, at night and in very poor weather. After finding the overturned scimitar, itself an amazing feat of flying at night in poor weather, in a steeply wooded area he hovered above it whilst the crew clambered aboard his Lynx to be flown back to Gornji Vakuf.

After the tour I was told that I'd been written up for the award of the Air Force Cross, but sadly for some reason didn't make the final cut. I did get to have supper with the then HRH Prince of Wales, now HRH King Charles 3$^{rd}$, at Middle Wallop during the AAC annual get together dinner. I shared his table with 2 generals, 2 brigadiers, and the Regimental Colonel. It was a great evening, which I still remember with pride.

*Figure 22 - A bit of High Jinks post Bosnia.*

# Chapter 15.

## Air Armaments MoD PE, London then Abbey Wood, Bristol.

Having enjoyed myself immensely commanding my squadron in Germany and Bosnia it was, sadly, payback time. The Army wanted reparation for the year spent studying for my master's degree and so I was informed that I would be posted to Air Armaments Branch in the MoD Procurement Executive to be part of the newly formed Apache Team, and responsible for certifying and buying the weapons we had selected to arm our version of the Apache helicopter. There would be no flying for me during this tour, but it turned out to be quite exciting anyway. This was a 3-year posting travelling backwards and forwards to America regularly to certify the UK's new Apache helicopter weapons and weapon control systems (as safe to UK standards) and then set up the contracts to buy CRV7 rockets, Hellfire missiles and 30mm cannon ammunition for the aircraft.

Hunting Engineering Ltd based just North of London were selected to be contract lead with all the US companies involved in producing the Hellfire anti-tank missile, and the 30mm ammunition for the cannon under the Apache nose, and the Canadian company which produced the CRV-7 rockets we had decided to buy instead of the American ones. They were a great team and incredibly responsive to our requests. The 3-year contract was for over £300 million, and I was responsible for making sure it was all spent wisely! Of course, being British, we didn't just want an off-the-shelf version of any of the armaments – we wanted our own version. In addition, in those days the government stipulated that we (*UK PLC Ltd*) understand everything about all armaments being bought from abroad and certified them ourselves as "safe to carry" on one of our expensive Apache helicopters and to fire too, if necessary. The British Ordnance Board were the people who did this back then and that meant I had to liaise with them over testing all the weapons we were buying in the States, attending technical and design conferences and test firings across the USA. Most of the US Trials were located in Redstone Arsenal's testing grounds at Huntsville in Alabama. I got to know this area well over the next 3 years and was lucky enough to be liaising with a US Marines Colonel who had also been to Kuwait/Iraq for the first war and better still was a helicopter pilot. We got on like a house on fire! The Americans were very secretive about how their weapons/armaments actually work – most of their international customers are sold the weapon with simple instructions such as "light blue touch paper and stand well back" and not allowed to know or understand much technical detail about them at all. That wasn't good enough for UK PLC, although they tried very hard to keep as much as possible to themselves. One day about 6 months into my tenure I was attending a technical conference in Phoenix Arizona where the British contingent was due to sign off on a design change for our Apache which involved the weapons. The radar guided Hellfire version (which we were buying alongside the laser guided version) was being discussed but the American team was being very cagey about the seeker head, its capabilities and how it worked. They produced a few diagrams which satisfied the aircraft engineers amongst the British team, but I realised what they were saying wasn't actually technically correct. It was highly technical and is probably still SECRET, so I won't allude exactly to what was being discussed, but as the meeting was at SECRET level (i.e. everyone there had been vetted and cleared to that level at least – I was top-secret cleared at that time) I stood up and challenged them and then explained why their diagrams were not correct. There was a massive silence and then I was asked to attend a side meeting with some of their experts. During that meeting they realised that I knew far more about how the missile worked than most of their own staff (due to my master's degree) and it was decided that there was no point further obscuring details about any of the weapons we were buying going forwards. This was a major victory and paved the way to an easy full UK certification of all the weapons on the Apache, and a long-term change in how the US weapons industry approached us in the UK for future projects.

On another visit to Huntsville my immediate boss (a charming RAF Group Captain) and his boss decided they would like to fly over and visit some of the experts and businesses I had been dealing with. My US Colonel contact arranged for us all to be taken out to the "Huntsville Gentlemen's Club" which was a well to do private dining and drinking club which all the local landlords and wealthy businessmen were members of a bit like a London gentleman's club. I was told that we needed jackets but no tie but somehow managed to turn this around in my head so that I told my bosses to bring a tie and don't bother with a jacket – this made sense to me as it was roasting in Alabama at that time of year and in an officer's mess in the UK we would have been in "planters order" – shirt sleeves and a tie! They flew in and we picked them up with about 2 hours to spare before we were expected at the Club. For some reason the subject of jackets came up and we realised they didn't have one (and neither did I). My American Colonel was the same size as one so he said we would drive to his house to collect one of his, and the other 2 including me would have to borrow one kept by the club for the exact purpose. For those who have seen the films "Southern Comfort" and "Deliverance" it will be easy to picture the scene as we drove what seemed like miles into the swamps of southern Alabama to pick up this jacket, in a pick-up truck with 4 hunting rifles racked up just above our heads. My 2 bosses wondered if they would get out alive, I'm sure. Arriving at the Club just in time I was forced to wear a white tuxedo jacket and my bosses' boss who was a lovely large-framed RAF Air Vice Marshal got a very loud check jacket. The 3 of us were probably the worst dressed British officers ever seen in Alabama! Dinner, however, was superb, a whole lobster each and a 12-ounce steak cooked to perfection, washed down with some fantastic Californian wines which must have cost at least $100 a bottle! The next morning, we were driven out onto the ranges at Redstone Arsenal and watched 5 hellfire missiles being fired (there were 5 different targeting modes for these missiles) and then my 2 bosses flew home happy – a perfect visit!

Coming back down to earth a few weeks later I had to fly back into Belfast City airport only 500m away from where I had been stationed during my first 4 months on operational tour back in the late 80's, to visit Shorts Missile Systems Ltd – we were looking at potentially purchasing their very fast Starstreak missile as an on-wing air defence mounted weapon for the Apache. It was very weird to be able to travel pretty much where we wanted in Belfast without being tooled up with personal weapons and body armour!

Trips were also regularly taken over to Cold Lake in northern Canada where we tested the Apache and its weapons in a rich Electronic Warfare environment to check firstly that the weapons wouldn't explode spontaneously and that they would actually work as advertised when we needed them to; and visits to Florida to visit Northrop Grumman (who made the radar seeker for the Hellfire RF missile) followed. All incredibly interesting and all classified so I can't say much more about those. This was a really rewarding 3 years – which ended with the purchase of all our stocks of Apache weapons being delivered safely and on time.

# Chapter 16.

**S**econd in Command - 1 Regiment AAC in Gutersloh, **Germany**.  Having completed an uneventful Gazelle Refresher at Middle Wallop in September 1998 I drove my family back out to Germany to take over my new position of second in command of 1 Regiment AAC – the same Regiment I had commanded my squadron in previously.

Unfortunately, since I had finished my tour commanding 661 Squadron the Regiment had slowly converted to Lynx only and lost its last Gazelles very soon after I arrived.  I wasn't able to wangle a place on a Lynx refresher, so I did very little flying during this tour.  The 3 years were pretty much uneventful with periods spent on exercise with HQ 1 UK Armoured Division as the aviation liaison officer responsible for arranging aviation support to the 3 fighting Brigades and making sure the routes flown at low level across the "battlefield" by Lynx and Gazelle were cleared through various layers of air defence assets, so that we didn't attempt to shoot our own helicopters down.  There were only 2 exceptions to this pretty normal life:  the first was a short period (8 weeks) where I stood in for the Commanding Officer and at one stage had to oversee the arrest by military police of one of my best mates who had been accused of illegal car buying and selling.  This was never proven.  At that stage my next posting had been agreed with Glasgow – I was to go and teach tactics at Warminster whilst my good friend was due to go to BATUS (British Army Training Unit Suffield), in Alberta, Canada to command the Gazelle flight which led the safety effort at the busiest and largest UK range complex in the World, and also teach aviation tactics from the air to the wider Army – his was a plum job, mine whilst interesting and fun, was not.  To my everlasting good fortune, the furore over the alleged illegal car buying meant my good friend was suddenly unable to go to Canada at the very last minute, and I had the task as his acting CO of informing Glasgow "that they had a significant problem", and after a pause for effect "that I had a solution"! Within 2 days I had confirmation that our posting allocations had been switched and I with my family were now off to Canada, where I would get another 2 years "in command" of a flying unit, and one of the plum postings for AAC Majors with loads of flying to boot – whoopee!

The second was arranging and then leading an adventurous training expedition to follow the GR5 through the alps all the way from Geneva to Nice – 400 miles on foot, ascending the equivalent of 3 Mt Everests en-route.

*Figure 23 – Mountain Leader - Ex Evian Diamond (walking the GR5).*

# Chapter 17.

**British Army Training Unit Suffield, Alberta, Canada - Officer Commanding 29 (BATUS) Flight AAC.** In August 2001 I flew out to Calgary via Vancouver to conduct a recce and handover at BATUS (British Army Training Unit Suffield) – a month flying virtually every day with Major Alex Haig (the outgoing Officer Commanding 29 Flight AAC) on a full exercise programme acting as safety aircraft and teaching tactics; all ultra-low level and great fun. Our role was to provide emergency CASEVAC for any exercising British troops who became injured or seriously sick whilst in Canada; and to provide a Directing Staff function to those whose tactical flying of the Gazelle was being honed ready for deployment on operations Worldwide, whilst also keeping a safety eye on the exercising infantry and armoured battlegroups from just above them. We could see further than ground-based safety staff in the undulating terrain of the prairies and observe when an errant infantry vehicle or tank was about to encroach on the safe firing arcs of our live artillery, infantry and tanks during their live-fire manoeuvres. The exercising Gazelles took part in "dry" (live action but simulated not live fire) exercises, live fire exercises and full scale TESEX (Tactical Engagement Simulated Exercises) simulated live fire exercises where all troops wore laser detecting sensors and all weapons were fitted with lasers instead of firing bullets or shells; and also, in providing CASEVAC to ground based troops during the Battlegroup or Brigade level exercises.

Having completed a full 5-week BATUS exercise cycle with Alex explaining all the intricacies (so I had experienced all the exercise scenarios firsthand) I flew back from Canada via Calgary on 01 September and started my Gazelle refresher course at Middle Wallop 2 days later. Having flown late into the night (on NVG revision sorties) on 9th and 10th September I was scheduled to "lift" at 1pm on the 11th and fly on instruments from the left-hand seat in the Gazelle for my final Gazelle Instrument Handling test – this as explained much earlier in the book is slightly more difficult than from the right-hand seat due to the instrument panel being offset to the right – for use by a right hand seat pilot. I had just walked into the REME 700 office to sign out my Gazelle (we check the 700 engineering log to see if everything on the aircraft is (a) serviced properly and (b) in working order – we can fly with lots of kit not functioning as long as we know about it beforehand) – when I looked up at the news feed from CNN playing live on the TV mounted on the wall above the counter…

…and the World changed forever.

Having watched the 2 hijacked US airliners fly into both towers and the immediate aftermath I then walked out and climbed into my Gazelle for my final check ride with the senior instructor. You can imagine the conversation throughout the otherwise completely uneventful flight and award of Master Green instrument rating again.

Two weeks later, after a period where the Americans (and Canadians) grounded all flights by airlines whilst they worked out how to prevent a similar attack happening again, I and my family flew from Heathrow to Calgary on 23rd September 2001 wondering if we would actually get there alive; at least we (the 2 grown-ups) felt that if it happened we would all die together, and the 2 youngsters wouldn't be parentless if we suffered the same fate as American Airlines Flight 11, American Airlines Flight 77, United Airlines Flight 175 and United Airlines Flight 93. Thankfully, after arriving safely at Vancouver and being picked up by a big minibus we arrived 4 hours later into Ralston, the small village in the middle of no-where which we would call home for the next 2 years – think "little house on the prairie" and that will give you a good idea!

Having had time to think about the entire exercise scenario I had flown through during my recce experience with Alex, I decided that I should make some improvements. Whilst based in Germany I had got used to replicating a number of callsigns from one Gazelle to make the exercises my Gazelle Flight and the whole Squadron were engaged in more realistic and thought this would go down well at BATUS as well. I also decided that we should make some of the exercises – involving the exercising Gazelles in an "advance to contact", a little more realistic by adding targets that continued to advance towards the exercising Gazelles once they had been spotted forcing the exercising Gazelles to move back tactically whilst still reporting their position and possible enemy intentions to the higher authority. Unfortunately, there were only a few sets of rail mounted targets available, they were only covering a move of up to 100m and were exceptionally expensive to site in the undulating ground. I wanted to force the Gazelle crews to move back at least 3 preferably up to 5 kilometers whilst continually reporting on the "enemy" advance as this would test their skills much more than simply engaging the targets with artillery once they had spotted them. So, I arranged for an extended series of pop-up targets to be dug in along an avenue of advance which the enemy might use following "dead" ground and not sticking to obvious routes or one speed. By using some of my soldiers in a land-rover hidden in the folds of ground to control the target's up/down mechanism by command wire I could raise and lower up to 20 tank silhouette type targets at will – making it look as though the enemy were advancing or retreating as I wished. This really tested the exercising Gazelle crews, especially when the "enemy" bypassed them and appeared so to speak "in their rear-view mirrors" by using dead ground.

Some of the crews coming through training at BATUS were likely to be headed out to Iraq if the second coalition war kicked off, and the Iraqi army had good air defence networks based on the Soviet model. UK based AAC crews were not used to operating in a non-permissive air defence environment at that time, so I decided to add in some realistic training to the initial simulated live fire training and TESEX scenarios. Having read up on soviet doctrine for man portable air defence weapons (manpads) and low level air defence of their battle group equivalents I added realism into the exercise scenarios and also ensured that if the pilots didn't ask their own ground forces they were flying over en-route to their area of operations for "air defence weapons tight" then I would occasionally tell one of the Gazelle pair on a discrete radio frequency to go silent and land so that the other Gazelle crew didn't know what had happened to them. This simulated them being shot down, either by enemy fire or occasionally by our own troops' air defence systems – exactly as happened to one unfortunate Gazelle during the 1982 Falklands conflict. These 2 enhancements to Alex's otherwise excellent exercise scenarios went down extremely well – at least after the bollocking the crews got from me for their initial cockups. The Gazelle crews learnt exceptionally quickly and after the $2^{nd}$ Gulf war I was very pleased to receive a couple of hand-written letters thanking me for producing such realistic training, which they felt had saved British aircrew's lives.

The live fire element of a Battlegroup's training at BATUS was partly strictly controlled but also allowed freedom of decision and action by the exercising troops. During live fire exercises the Gazelles were usually training with artillery strikes against fixed and "moving" target arrays on secure range areas, whereas the remainder of the ground-based battlegroup were put through their paces on a series of exercises against targets controlled by the other BATUS directing staff. They practiced everything from advance to contact, mounted and dismounted attacks and defence and specialist operations such as minefield breaching, river crossing and bridge laying with attendant forming and break out from bridgeheads. The pace was frenetic, and the realism sky high. Whilst the exercising Gazelles were kept safely out of the way my callsign "5" and my second in command "5B" would be intimately involved with the battlegroups, ensuring that they didn't accidentally target any of our own exercising troops with live weapons. The issue was that the ground was so undulating that it was very easy for vehicles and men to get slightly lost, and to advance or retreat at different speeds which led to them accidentally moving into the live-fire arcs of the main body of the exercising Battlegroup. They were involved in firing live ammunition against targets throughout their manoeuvre battle. By flying above the main elements of the Battlegroup – for instance the tanks, at around 100' agl we could see into all the folds of ground and check the tanks weren't about to fire their main guns at friendly vehicles. This was pretty exciting flying, although incredibly sick making for any passenger, tight turns swooping and diving whilst keeping an eagle eye on all elements of the battlegroup was very tiring flying, but hugely rewarding. Whenever a minefield or river crossing was about to be put in, we would provide the final "all clear" checking all troops had cleared the danger area before the python lane clearance explosive charge was fired. Of course, with a full battlegroup of armoured vehicles charging around and dismounted infantry attacks going in left right and centre there were the occasional mishaps. The exercising Gazelle flight were responsible for providing CASEVAC throughout their time on the prairie and the live-fire exercise period was the most likely time they would be used. Each element of the Army had its own directing staff at BATUS, usually a Major who had already commanded his sub-unit

(Squadron or Company). Some elements (infantry, armour, artillery and aviation) also had a Captain as side-stick along with a few very experienced Warrant Officers. Any of the BATUS directing staff could call for a "STOP, STOP, STOP" at any time they thought an accident was about to occur or had occurred and all motion and firing would instantly cease across the whole exercise area when the call went out. We were known by our callsigns – mine was "5", my Captain rank assistant "5B" and my Warrant Officer "5C". The Battlegroup would go onto radio silence and the AAC Gazelle flight go into CASEVAC mode day or night until stood down. Usually, one exercising helicopter would fly and pick up the battlegroup doctor whilst the other would fly to the casualty, land, strip the left-hand seat out if a stretcher was needed and then plan their subsequent potential trip to Medicine Hat hospital. Occasionally my Gazelles would also get involved if the weather was below safe limits for normal flying (see later), or there were mass casualties. One day I was circling above the artillery section firing their 3 AS90s in support of an infantry live fire attack and looking down I suddenly saw smoke pouring out of the AS90 turret, followed immediately by its crew of 4 soldiers. The top of the turret is a long way up (around 3m above ground) and one of the crew fell badly apparently breaking his ankle. It didn't stop him running like a hare for around 150m before diving to the ground as the turret blew off the chassis – burning propellant charge residue in the barrel had ignited a bag charge for the 120mm ammunition as it was being loaded into the gun's breach causing a major fire. Luckily, he was the only casualty. The other interesting incident involved a Challenger tank which managed to roll over off the side of a bailey bridge which had been built over a small creek on one of the range areas. Landing upside down the crew managed to get inside the turret before it landed, and the operation to get the tank out of the river lasted quite a few hours. Again, all the crew survived pretty much unscathed.

When out on the ranges with the exercising gazelle crews I would normally walk the 5km across the prairie to work (whatever the weather, sometimes minus 40 degrees Celsius and drifting powder snow) getting to the hangar at around 03:00. Taking off 20 minutes before first light, I would land alongside the exercising troops night bivouac on the prairie at first light and listen in as their commander gave their exercise orders to his/her men. Then off we would go, and I would watch, control enemy actions to test the exercising gazelle crews and critique their response to the exercise scenario. We would only stop for a suck of avgas and to scoff my packed lunch when I could take a quick break. I would have a very full day often flying 6 or 7 hours, very tiring in the cold or heat and constantly watching what was going on around me. One hot summer day, flying with the doors removed, we suffered more than usual from "may bugs" slamming into the Perspex canopy as we flew along. Landing for fuel I looked around for another rag to clean the mess off the canopy and realised we didn't have any left, there had been so many bugs smeared over the Perspex throughout the day. I needed to clean the canopy as I could hardly see out – so I grabbed the only clean article left in the cockpit – my brown paper sandwich bag, and wetting it started wiping the bugs off all over the canopy. Having got rid of most of them I then rinsed off the mess and waited for the canopy to clear of water evaporating off in the heat. But the canopy didn't clear! It stayed very dirty and on close inspection I realised it was covered in millions of scratches and swirls – all caused by the abrasive brown paper bags! The £30k canopy had to be replaced, which was very embarrassing but I learnt a valuable lesson – never use paper to clean sunglasses or any other plastic article.

I had some fun and interesting trips in Canada; Wildfire extinguishing – using the BATUS gazelle in a low hover to make a wind break and drive the flames to extinguish themselves as their progress across the prairie grass was halted by the downdraft from the rotors; flying in the Rocky mountains, only a few thousand feet high above the prairie, but prairies were at 6000' agl, learning to fly using both the external references but also blending instrument flying into the same picture to ensure what my eyes were telling me was level terrain actually was – this because when flying low in the mountains the only thing we could see was the rock in front of us and a strata layer within the rock at an angle to horizontal could appear to be level, causing a crash.  I managed to bend a Gazelle main landing skid on a rock hidden by deep snow on 26 November 2002 when attempting to land to pick up the Royal Engineer directing staff (Major Nick Sealy-Thompson RE, callsign "6") miles from anywhere to fly him back to the base … flying back 60 nautical miles at just over hover speed and sitting in the hover being refueled by hand for a further 40 minutes whilst my REME aviation engineers decided whether I could land on the skids or must belly land on a pile of sandbags; a MEDEVAC from an pick up site 40 miles north of my base in thick fog – our normal visibility limit was 1000m visibility with a minimum cloud-base of 300' above the ground, this was more like 100m in thick fog with cloud (fog) on the deck but the guy had apparently had a heart attack and a doctor was over 2 hours away by road. I flew out very low level at a fast hover speed to pick up the doctor mid route and then found the casualty, taking him to Medicine Hat hospital before flying back home in slightly better (legal) weather.  The Army aviation standards officer who was visiting to check our flying at the time gave me a major bollocking for busting legal weather limits whilst forgetting to write *"authorised below normal weather limits"* in my authorisation sheet – then smiling, gave me another "above the average" grading as a Squadron commander.  One of the most challenging trips off the block were a couple of long-distance transits across the empty prairie taking BATUS commander (callsign "9") to visit training at Edmonton, we had fuel for only 5 minutes longer than the trip should take. Of course, we made it - just! Landing in the middle of the river Saskatchewan for a coffee break whilst flying a doors off low level recce with the Royal Armoured Corps DS (James Goodwin, callsign "2") and flying the unit's families across the prairie were cream on the cake. I also got to fly the Medicine Hat Rodeo Princesses (3 very pretty young ladies) into Ralston at the start of the annual Rodeo in my Gazelle dropping them in the area in front of the crowds; almost my last ever sortie in a Gazelle. I achieved the sought-after accolade of 2000 hours of flying in command of one of Her Majesty's army helicopters together with the ritual soaking and 2 bottles of chilled champers – a fitting end (I thought) to my flying career on one of my last flights in Canada.

*Figure 30 - a Ritual Soaking and ride in a fun helicopter marking my 2000 hours in command of Army helicopters.*

Oh... I also got promoted to Lieutenant Colonel and was given just 2 weeks' notice to pack up, hand over the BATUS flight and turn up in Wilton near Salisbury for my next job.

*Figure 24 - With my son, Hugo & a bottle for each 1000 hours - note he's already learnt to hold firmly onto the Champagne!*

# Chapter 18.

**Management Consultant (!) with McKinsey & Company PLC**.  Having returned to the UK and got my family settled into a married quarter in Wilton I hit the ground running.  Approximately 30 newly promoted Lieutenant Colonels, Wing Commanders (RAF) and Commanders (RN) were posted into a new tri-service unit, and the first task was to undergo training with McKinsey & Co based in St James, London to learn how to become a management consultant.  The 30 officers were from maintenance and logistic units in the main, with a few specialists such as EOD engineers and aviators thrown into the mix.  Our tasks were to make the logistic and maintenance procedures carried out by the Navy, Army and RAF "leaner" i.e. more efficient and effective.  We were to learn how to spot wasteful practices and then design and implement changes to long standing practices to get rid of the wasted time, effort and money which was endemic at the time.  As a non-helicopter engineer - even if I did have a batchelor's degree and a master's degree in engineering disciplines, I was not a practicing engineer and had never been involved in helicopter maintenance, so this was going to be "interesting" to say the least.  Challenging some highly experienced engineers into changing their ways was the main crux of the job, most were brilliant at accepting new methods, some less so.  My specific task once trained in management consultancy techniques was to go and look at how 7 Battalion REME maintained our Lynx helicopters and Apache helicopters in their main engineering base (known as "depth workshops") at Wattisham in Suffolk and also maintenance of both aircraft types in their front-line units.  For the Apache we would also look at how they were rearmed and refueled hoping to cut down the time taken to conduct such an evolution in between strike missions.  McKinsey & Co had recently been involved in looking at 2 operations which had similarities – the fast moving changing of tyres and refueling of a Grand Prix racing car (I think they worked with McLaren but am not certain) and with making NHS operating theatres run more efficiently so they could complete more medical operations each day. These two examples were used to teach us how to approach problems and after about 3 months training off we went – let loose on the engineering and logistics elements of all 3 Services. It was an enjoyable challenge and I am pleased that I (and the REME engineers who were so willing to be challenged) managed to increase the efficiency of Wattisham Apache and Lynx maintenance by around 25%, a significant figure as it increased the number of aircraft available in front line by that amount and also reduced the time taken to maintain them at front line, e.g. every 25 hours and 50 hours of flying by around 30%. Not a bad result. After 3 years of long-distance weekly commuting, I was pleased with the improvements in all the units I had worked with, but very happy to be able to move back to a more typical aviation qualified job for my next posting.

# Chapter 19.

## Chief Of Staff (COS) Army Aviation Centre Middle Wallop.

The Army Aviation Centre at Middle Wallop (where I had trained to fly quite a few years before) was headed up by an AAC full Colonel. As his Chief of Staff (or COS) I was responsible for running the Army Aviation Centre at Middle Wallop effectively and efficiently, and it was a full-on job. I was responsible for producing and resourcing training plans for AAC soldiers from basic training through all their specialist courses needed to teach them how to man, fuel, rearm and manage the fighting units in the field army, and then onto cadres for promotion all the way up to Warrant Officer. In addition, I had to provide the training centre with all the resources they needed to bring new young officers and qualified soldiers through the pilot training I had seen as a young lieutenant, but on the Squirrel helicopter which had replaced the Gazelle as our initial trainer, then through conversion onto Gazelle, Lynx, Bell 212 or Apache. I designed and developed an excel based planning tool which crunched the numbers to tell my boss exactly how many instructors of each type (flying, weapons, communications and skill at arms) and all the other resources we needed depending on the required throughput of students on each course each year. This took the guesswork out of manning and resourcing the school and meant we could justify demands for increases in manning, supplies or costs against otherwise unrealistic totals for training required by some staff officer in HQ Land. Unfortunately, this meant I was too busy to do much flying apart from a little bit of liaison flying around the country visiting field army units in a Squirrel.

I'd been going to see my kids play sport at their junior school for at least a term at weekends when I worked out that one of the other dads, who I often chatted to was something different from the normal. Quiet, very fit and no taller than myself, he exuded a quiet confidence and was often away for weeks at a time. His daughter and mine shared a dormitory so it was natural that we'd chat together on the side-lines, but we never talked about work. We became good friends. Just after my kids left that school, I bumped into General Gary Coward (late AAC) who was in charge of the Joint Helicopter Command and had previously been my old Commanding Officer in 1 Regiment Army Air Corps when I returned from Bosnia to Germany with 661 Squadron. I had met General Gary socially and whilst chatting had told him that having gained masses of operational experience in my younger days, I was feeling out of touch with the younger officers and soldiers around me because my last operational tour had been some years previously; they were all gaining up-to-date operational experience in Iraq and now Afghanistan, and I felt professionally left out. I asked to be allowed to command the Afghanistan Op HERRICK Aviation Unit (a regimental sized group consisting of Army Air Corps, RAF and RN helicopters) for a 6-month tour. General Gary told me that sadly that wasn't going to be possible as he had made an edict when he took over as Commander Joint Helicopter Command that the commanding officer of that organisation must be a current CO of one of the 3 Services' aviation units in the Joint Helicopter Command at the time. I wasn't – I was in a staff position within the AAC, as Chief of Staff of the AAC Centre. Damn! He did remember though that he had said I did a fantastic job in Bosnia and should be allowed to command an AAC regiment hopefully on operations; and said he would make some enquiries. About a week later he called me to his office and asked if I'd like to command another operational aviation unit, and if so, would I prefer Iraq or Afghanistan. He had run my name past the current operational commanders and my previous experience had been discussed. They were happy for me to command a unit in whichever theatre I wanted. At that stage (2008) Iraq had been going on for some time and I felt I would be better placed and more relevant with my experience to take on the relatively new Afghanistan role. Luckily, he wholeheartedly agreed.

# Chapter 20.

**Afghanistan - Commander - UK Aviation Unit - Operation Herrick.** Immediately Commander JHC notified me that I was going to Afghanistan I set about sorting out some training for myself. The first thing I wanted to do was fly an Apache from the weapon operator's or front seat aircraft commander / pilot's position. I wanted to do this for 2 reasons – I knew exactly what all the weapons were capable of having purchased and been intimately involved in their UK certification some 10 years or so ago, but I wanted to be certain that when an AAC pilot said he could positively identify a target individual or vehicle during daylight and at night I wanted to be absolutely certain, as I would be held responsible if the Apache hit the wrong targets whilst supporting troops during my tour. I also wanted to see what it was like to fly an Apache in direct support of ground forces so that I could gauge the risk to the aircraft during standard attack manoeuvres – the Apache experts on the aviation standards team based at Middle wallop had just been teaching these techniques out in theatre and so were perfectly placed to allow me this training if I could persuade the JHC commander that it was necessary. In theatre I would be deciding what attack profile would be best suited to provide optimum support to the soldiers on the ground during any action supported by our Apache helicopters. Apart from a bit of liaison flying in the Squirrel I had done no other flying during my tour at Middle Wallop, so I really wanted to fly from the front seat (the aircraft commander or weapons system operator seat) of the Apache; but there was a significant problem in allowing pilots unqualified on type to fly the early marks of the Apache from the front seat. A system called BUCS needed to be operated in certain scenarios with very little warning, and for some reason the early Apache only have the BUCS button on the front seat aircraft commander's collective stick. The instructor flying with me would not have access to this button as we were separated by a wall of armour-plated composites and glass! Not pressing the correct button immediately without hesitation if required would end in losing control of the Apache and a nasty crash – guaranteed! However, Commander JHC could see my reasoning and agreed my request. After a couple of trips in the simulator to train me how to use the BUCS button if necessary I flew day and night sorties from the front (commander's) seat in order for me (as air weapon release authority in my forthcoming operational tour) to be completely up to speed with what the Apache sensors and pilots flying missions in Afghanistan in support of UK troops could see and distinguish, day and night.

*Figure 25 - After my first Apache "c/s UGLY" flight.*

In the end I flew 5 sorties in the Apache, 3 day and 2 night, spending around 11 hours in the air – it is a marvelous fighting helicopter – very easy to fly, but difficult to fight due to the plethora of data available to the crew and the multitude of weapons buttons festooned around the collective lever, none of them lit and all to be learned off by heart during aircrew training by feel only.

In addition to flying the Apache I also arranged to visit the troops I would be supporting at their base. I turned up and found the offices being used by the unit who were going to be deployed for the whole of my tour as well. Having walked in I shook hands with a couple of tough looking men and asked if the Sergeant Major (SSM) or Officer Commanding was around. The OC had been called off at short notice to a higher priority meeting, but the guys said the SSM would be along shortly. Imagine my surprise when WO2 Carl M[40] walked in and with a grin introduced himself to me as SSM of the unit I'd be working with. We had been mates for around 7 years, but he had never told me his rank or which unit he worked in. Once the rest of the guys had stopped laughing their socks off at my surprise we got down to business and started to discuss tactics etc. I asked about training and was told I could get some pursuit and evasion driving training, which was particularly vital as I was going to be driving in and around Kabul regularly, and some communications revision work in a weeks' time, followed by a week-long trip out to a desert exercise in about 3 weeks, where the unit were going to be practicing TTPs, Chinook evolutions and some work from high mobility vehicles. They also said I needed to

---

[40] Carl was promoted to Captain during my tour in Afghanistan. He was a first-class example of the elite Royal Marine – strong, resolute, compassionate and a real thinking soldier. He was an excellent mate. Unfortunately, he died during a subsequent tour in Afghanistan. I attended his funeral in along with hundreds of military and civilian mourners.

get my first aid training up to speed and qualify as a specialist marksman as I was going to be out on the ground in some scenarios in Afghanistan operating both on foot occasionally as well as in vehicles and from helicopters or C130s and they needed to know I wouldn't accidentally shoot them if we were in a contact situation. I relished this part of the training because I have always been a good shot – in fact I was an Army marksman on the pistol, rifle and GPMG machinegun! Driver training was great fun – I have always loved driving and there were 2 elements to this part of the training. Firstly, as I was likely to be driving vehicles in and around various locations in Afghanistan, I needed to be able to get myself out of an ambush situation and know how to react should my vehicle be hit by an IED. I would be driving or carried in either military or armoured civilian vehicles, and these were heavy, and we needed to remember not to try to shoot through the windows if we were engaged by small arms fire as the bullets would then be ricocheting around inside the armoured vehicle, probably killing ourselves! I also brushed up on how to report on my location when moving by vehicle in a high threat area, I hadn't done that since Northern Ireland. In addition to this we were drilled in anti-ambush drills and learnt methods of extracting from being under effective enemy fire. Fun parts included putting down covering fire when targets popped up in front of us simulating a road-block, learning how to execute a J-turn to get out of a "hot" area quickly along with polishing my handbrake turns and ramming our way through a vehicle road-block without destroying our own vehicle. Driving passed with flying colours it was off to the ranges next. We had to pass the elite infantry pistol and rifle weapon tests, gaining a higher percentage of hits and at a much greater distance than I was used to. Being effective with a pistol is much harder than in the movies! However, I was having a problem with the new pistol at 5m – I couldn't hit the target accurately half the time, I always hit it but not in the centre where I was aiming for. One of the instructors on the range was a long-retired veteran of the parachute regiment, and he walked up to me saying "*Boss, are you a marksman on the Colt 45?*" (the Army issue pistol at the time). I thought he was taking the piss but answered in the affirmative. He grinned and said he thought so – shooting the new pistol required a completely different technique. Once he had taught me the revised grip and stance, I started hitting all the targets all the time and passed my test with ease. No problems with the rifle either, which was a lovely weapon, light, accurate, relatively short which suited my small frame and quick to bring into action.

I deployed to the pre-deployment desert exercise flying via Abu Dhabi, then driving up into the mountains to where the next training evolution was to take place.

One of the first evolutions was to get out onto a plain north of the coastal mountain range with a couple of chinooks. First of all, we used just one, then introduced the second into a simulated mission. The objective was to get the troops safely onto the ground very close to the target with as little warning as possible. Both chinooks were flown aggressively to make it difficult for any enemy to fire either a gun or an RPG at us during the procedure. Bristling with 2 miniguns and a GPMG the chinook had been used for years as a method of getting troops onto target. I sat in the jump seat just behind the 2 pilots, in the gunner station beside the open side door, and on the tail ramp whilst the crews practiced these manoeuvres alternating between the 2 chinooks time after time whilst we practiced. What I noticed was that the crews flew incredibly professionally and the whole evolution worked like clockwork with one slight issue. The troops were sitting in the back of the chinooks whist the aircraft were "thrown about" quite severely to ensure targeting them from the ground was as difficult as possible, but they couldn't see out and therefore most of them were being made to feel very sick, just before we needed them to charge out of the chinook and assault the target, perhaps under effective return fire from the target. Whilst the troops didn't complain I could see that this degraded their performance for the first few minutes on the ground. So, I had to make my first operational decision and told the chinook pilots to practice with slightly less aggressive maneuvering and approaching the target location from a different angle in order to ensure the assault team were at peak performance when they hit the ground. The crews adjusted their flying accordingly, and the assault troops stopped being sick. The aircraft were still being thrown around to minimise the likelihood of being hit by incoming fire, but the operational effectiveness of the whole evolution jumped significantly, and I got a chance to meet with and fly with the crews who would be working for me in Afghanistan building a relationship of mutual trust and understanding before we deployed.

Another evolution practiced during training in the desert was insertion to a remote location by C130 Hercules transport aircraft. I would have 2 of these excellent and flexible transport aircraft at my disposal during my tour in Afghanistan. During training we had the opportunity of conducting some sport parachuting from the C130. Sitting on the tailgate of the Hercules whilst it flew at around 10,000 feet above the ground with only a dispatcher's belt to keep me from falling out of the aircraft, I cleared the troops to jump and then stood on the edge to watch them freefall for varying times before opening their chutes to land. One of the boys offered me a spare parachute on a daytime drop – I have to say I was sorely tempted but reason got the better of me – if I had injured myself there would have been hell to pay and I would probably be replaced as Air and Aviation Commander. Not something I wanted to happen! The Hercules flew out into an ad-hoc desert strip recced by unmanned air vehicle and map appreciation, to set up a refueling location which in Afghanistan could also host an Apache Forward Arming and Refueling Position. We then practiced long-range low-level flights by helicopter, flying nap of the earth for miles across the desert. All in all, great fun and really useful training, where the aircrew and the assault troops got to know me and realise that I knew my stuff and could be counted upon to utilise my skill sets and experience to provide as much aviation support as possible, safely minimising risk, whatever the situation we faced in theatre. At the end of the week, I flew back home via Abu Dhabi. We had been full-on for the 7 days, working day and night to ensure techniques and practices and SOPs were all clear, understood by all and most importantly – likely to be effective when facing the Taliban in the non-permissive environment of Afghanistan. On landing at Heathrow, I then headed for Northwood where after a night's sleep in the Mess I was briefed on the latest situation in Afghanistan and the surrounding countries by the Permanent Joint HQ staff. On top of working within Afghanistan from within theatre I was also in command of any air or aviation assets assigned to missions in the Middle to Far East during my tour, so I needed a lot of briefing on potential threats to UK nationals and potential operations across this wide area. A quick train ride took me into London to be briefed by my out-of-theatre boss and sign the Official Secrets Act. After that I visited the Foreign Office and DEFRA to be given their spin on what was happening and likely to happen during my tour. Amazing!

# Chapter 21.

## On the Ground (and in the Air) in Afghanistan.

After a week on leave I packed my bags and headed down to Middle Wallop at "Oh my god-o-clock" to draw my personal weapons; the pistol having been couriered over from the assault troops base. Then I was driven with a couple of others back past home to Brize Norton where we expected to board and fly out at 0400 the next day. Brize was, as always, complete and utter chaos. Senior RAF officers were nowhere to be seen and the lowest rank RAF airmen seemed to enjoy making the austere environment as unwelcoming and as painful as possible for the hundreds of Army soldiers and officers passing through their "kingdom". I had a tight schedule ahead of me with handover from my predecessor scheduled to start within minutes of my arrival in Southeastern Afghanistan. Prior to that I had to fly to Bastion and then cross-deck from Tristar to Hercules with all my kit. I only had 3 days to take over the operation – in two remote locations; the first where my HQ was located in Southeastern Afghanistan along with most of the assault troops, and my allocated aircraft fleet. The Reaper Squadron occupied the next dispersal pan and the UK Harrier squadron was around 100m away. The AAC Apache Helicopters flew out of their own base at BASTION, only around 20 minutes flying time from the green zone where most of our operations would be taking place. The second location was in Northeastern Afghanistan where UK military helicopter pilots drawn from the 3 services flew the choppers operated by the Afghan Air Force. Both were complicated operations and I needed to get fully up to speed with both locations and meet the teams during the 3-day handover. Of course, the RAF weren't going to let that go to plan and at around 23:00 on my planned eve of departure I was told I had been bumped off the Tristar and would fly a day late. There being no senior RAF officers around I called the duty Ops watch officer at HQ Land and asked them to intervene. Unfortunately, by the time they managed to speak to someone sensible the Tri-Star had left, so my planned 3-day handover was now down to 2! You couldn't make it up – any soldier would have gladly given up his/her seat for me as they were all going to sit around for a couple of days at Bastion waiting to start their in-theatre training package – I didn't need to do this as our training package in the UK and then in the desert was far more stringent and wide ranging – I was 100% ready to hit the ground running! Eventually, a day late, I scrambled out of the Hercules at my new HQ location and looked for my predecessor. Not so easy when thousands of troops were milling about, so he wore his RAF beret and I my AAC one which was highly unusual in Afghanistan, ensuring we saw each other immediately my feet hit the tarmac. Grabbing me out of the queue he told me someone would get my gear including my rifle as and we needed to push off asap. I was wearing my pistol already and he handed me 3 full magazines. So, within seconds of arriving I failed to follow the well learnt SOP of anyone in the Army around RAF movers and that was to never lose sight of your kit! Thankfully it later turned up in the lines and my rifle was booked into the armoury. Unlike most troops we were allowed to keep our sidearm continually throughout the tour, drawing our rifle from the armoury just outside the HQ building whenever we were leaving the base. Having blasted around the sprawling camp we entered the compound which had its own secure perimeter within the base and headed into the HQ complex – 2 inflatable double skin tents one of which housed around 15 staff officers and specialists siting at banks of computers and screens providing the hub for planning and monitoring all specialist operations in theatre, and one for the assault squadron themselves where they got ready for individual missions. A quick round of introductions followed and a visit to the green slime tent – where most of the intelligence used by the troops came into the compound. The Intelligence Corps (Green Slime) staff were superb, collating and constantly updating evidence and intelligence on a large number of targets from sources inside and outside Afghanistan.

# Chapter 22.

## Counter Insurgency (COIN) Ops - Op HERRICK.

For most of the operations where assault troops were inserted onto the ground, I provided a balanced aviation package designed to enhance the likelihood of mission success. Any coalition troops on the ground in Afghanistan could call for immediate CAS (Close Air Support) from the nearest fast air if they were involved in a TIC ("Troops in Contact"), but during my tour there were so many "contacts" on coalition troops that fast air support could not be guaranteed for most of our missions. However, for some pre-planned operations I did provide fixed wing fast air support directly tasked to support the mission, which meant they would not be called off to support other troops unless all hell was breaking loose elsewhere. Armed initially during my tour with 500lb free fall bombs, and later laser guided bombs the Harriers or Tornado were extremely useful as we could get a "picture" relayed from their weapon targeting pods into the command centre – another real time set of eyes giving enhanced target identification or increased /wide area situational awareness. Occasionally, early in the tour, Reaper or Predator support would drop out usually due to the limited number in theatre during the last few months of 2008, and the constant pressure for overwatch for the army whenever there was an IED or TIC. When that happened the only situational awareness enhancer, we could call upon was from the UK Harrier Force, who luckily were hangered just a few hundred metres away from my chinook dispersal, and for most of my tour were manned by RN pilots. They of course were hell bent on supporting their own brethren the Royal Marines whenever they could. To be fair, the RAF squadron which followed them, and unfortunately suffered the well-publicised Harrier crash and ejection on the main runway at Kandahar during the second half of my tour were just as dedicated. *Only we constantly made sure to wind them up that they weren't as good of course.* The Predator and Reaper gave me and the assault troop's commander direct oversight of the target and provided vital situational awareness of what was going on in the surrounding and immediate areas. I could watch the progress of the mission on the ground using the sensors fitted to the predator / Reaper and engage targets as necessary using the Apache's 30mm cannon, 76mm rockets fitted with a variety of warheads including anti-armour and flechete which was a series of 96 small tungsten darts, or eventually[41] Hellfire missiles launched by the Apache or Hellfire dropped by the Reaper UAV. I also had the ability to task the Chinook door gunners to provide direct support with the 2 General Electric M134 Miniguns mounted in the forward firing ports. Occasionally I was able to task the US AC130 Spectre gunship. This was an awesome bit of kit with a M137 105mm cannon, and an L60 40mm Bofors cannon. Flying above the target area I could bring down supporting direct fires at any time day or night with incredible accuracy.

The Hellfire used in Afghanistan could be fitted with an anti-tank dual warhead designed to blow through explosive reactive armour and other defenses seen recently in Russian tanks in the Ukraine conflict, and it could also be fitted with a modified payload missile which used an explosive to shatter a cylinder made up of rings of fragments in a blast and anti-personnel function. We always used the laser guidance seeker head version. The RAF at the time were trying to get Brimstone cleared for use in Afghanistan and as the command centers which cleared the use of all air launched missions were manned by RAF personnel there was a political game being played to prevent Hellfire from getting a handhold or head start in theatre. When I arrived in theatre, we

---

[41] For the first 3 months of our tour, we were not allowed to utilise the best weapon fitted to the Apache, the Hellfire ATGW.

were allowed to use artillery to pound a target but not Hellfire to surgically strike a group of insurgents or building because (in my mind) of this political battle led by the RAF to dominate the future airspace support package. I eventually realised this was why we were continually being denied the use of Hellfire as a strike weapon against targets even where there was negligeable risk of collateral damage. So, I got on one of my C130 and travelled to Kabul where I visited the Combined Air Operations Cell (CAOC) to personally deliver a hard hitting "Paper" I had written (and had co-signed by the assault team commander) to the Air Vice Marshall in charge of the CAOC which at the same time hit the MOD back in the UK. This Paper pointed out the utility of Hellfire, which could be aimed with exacting precision, and called off the target even at the last few seconds by moving the laser spot to a safe area, against the use of artillery which is indiscriminate and whose flight path and impact point cannot be altered once it has left the gun or rocket barrel, often some 30 to 45 seconds before impact. My Paper won the day, and we (and other coalition troops) were henceforth allowed to call on Hellfire in support – a complete game changer as surgical strikes became the normal. Later, Javelin a shoulder launched anti-tank & anti-bunker missile was also brought into use.

Hellfire was henceforth used against buildings occasionally in the blast frag role, against vehicles which had failed to stop when required and against groups of insurgents where the risk of fratricide or accidentally injuring non-combatants or other collateral damage was negligeable.

Day and night insertions were used, to drop the assault troops often some distance away from the target location and sometimes right up close just out of effective small arms range. Often these locations – usually a couple of compounds in the middle of an open desert area were a long way out from other habitation in the desert and were used for sleeping only, with the enemy HVT then travelling back to the green zone in the morning to carry on trying to ambush UK and other soldiers with IEDs, the most common form of Taliban assault during my 6 months in theatre. The issue with flying nap of the earth at night in those days was that the depth perception achieved with twin tube NVG in low light conditions was poor. As pilots, we developed big necks because we constantly had to scan from side to side whilst flying nap-of-the earth in order to pick up clues as to how high we were (we also used radar altimeters for this) and how fast we were moving over the ground. Looking at the flat green picture produced by the early generation NVG tubes (even Gen 4 wasn't brilliant) which was subsequently fed into our eyes it was incredibly hard to work out how fast you are moving, and scanning helped in this.

In the days before we had Hellfire cleared for use, we carried out a couple of missions that required support from the American C-130 Spectre as the target area was out of range of any coalition artillery. Using the aircraft's 40mm cannon, and 105mm gun the missions were completed successfully.

There was a significant small arms risk against the chinook whenever flying close to Taliban fighters or compounds where they and their support elements were hiding. One of the key roles of UK assault teams was to use the Chinooks to allow the troops to assault targets clear of any urban areas and allow the capture of the individuals thereby gaining useful intelligence; hopefully cutting down on the appalling number of British soldiers being blown up and maimed or killed in the Green Zone in 2008 and 2009. Back in Northern Ireland some 20 years ago we used a Lynx or sometimes 2 to provide a "stop" team in support of the infantry and PSNI against potential terrorists moving from one location to another. The biggest risk was that one or more of the potential terrorists would open fire on the Lynx from close quarters, although I believe this never happened. In Afghanistan the insurgents would try to engage the chinooks with RPG or machine guns fired from their locations as the choppers closed in on the drop off location. It was only a matter of time before they were successful, and as each chinook contained 4 aircrew and up to 30 Royal Marine troops the cost would be very high indeed. I decided to utilise the firepower carried by the Chinooks as a direct strike weapon to neutralise the enemy from the outset in areas where there was no risk of collateral damage. The M134 Minigun could fire around 4000 x 7.62 rounds a minute very accurately. It was possible to "walk" the stream of tracers included within the standard load for the minigun accurately onto any target once the minigun began firing. The RAF door gunners were able to learn how to suppress any Taliban firing point as the choppers approached and landed close to their target whereby the occupants were then given a chance to give themselves up to the assaulting troops with minimised risk to the aircraft. This method was cleared by both HQ Land and HQ JHC before being used in anger. It was incredibly successful and allowed the troops to get closer to their target before deploying onto the ground.

I made sure that if we were to strike a group travelling within a vehicle that it was done away from any habitation, partly to prevent any collateral damage from our own fires but also to minimise the risk of the aircraft being effectively targeted during the assault. If assaulting a compound or compounds I ensured that the risk during approach and departure from landing sites was minimised by careful planning using maps and satellite pictures; and the mini-gun toting chinooks acted in mutual support throughout. Occasionally enemy fighters managed to evade the landing troops and we would mount up to attempt to capture them after the target had been cleared. On one occasion the 2 chinooks were sucked into the edge of the Green Zone whilst chasing 2 separate individuals on the edge of the Green Zone[42]. A fast-flowing gun battle ensued with the 2 chinooks flying around a series of compounds and a market area using their miniguns with multiple fighters streaming out of the Green Zone supporting the 2 escaping Taliban with rifle and RPG fires. A total of 5 RPG were fired towards the Chinooks and when one passed within 100m I called the chinooks off. They disengaged immediately and returned safely to base. That was the only time I had to cancel a mission once it was started but it proved the concept of having overwatch from senior aviation officer to mitigate any heat of the battle decisions taken by the engaged aircrew, or by assault troops which put the aircraft in too much danger. In fact, during my 6-month tour I always sat up in the HQ overseeing the mission unfold or accompanied the aircraft in the Chinook jump seat depending on what was going on. This meant that I could over-ride the assaulting troops commander when I felt it necessary for the safety of the aircraft. The fact that I never had to "pull the plug" from this point of view showed just how well integrated my air wing was with the assault troops, and how much we trusted each other to get the job done as safely and effectively as possible throughout my tour. Of course, this was combat, and it was inherently dangerous, but a large part of my job was to maximise the effectiveness of the assaulting troops and minimise the risk to my aircrew and the troopers when aboard my aircraft. It was a challenging role but made so much easier by the Royal Marines fantastic attitude towards me and my men & women aviators throughout my tour.

We had an ever-changing list of targets we were interested in,

---

[42] The "Green Zone" was the fertile river plain area in central Afghanistan over which most of the UK element of ISAF fought the Taliban.

and pretty close to top of the list were those who were bomb makers and taught others how to do the same. Sometimes a foot patrol by coalition infantry or various other intelligence led methods or sources showed that a building was being used as a bomb factory, and we had 2 options – destroy it at the time or wait and hope to catch the bomb maker and possibly a bomb teacher in the building at some time in the near future. At this time in the Afghanistan campaign the biggest cause of coalition troops injury and death was through IEDs, either victim initiated (such as a pressure plate) or command initiated (which could be simply using a string with 2 steel washers acting as a switch or using more sophisticated methods such as a mobile phone or walkie-talkie) to set them off when a patrol was within lethal range. We would set up remote observation and watch to be sure the HVT we were interested in was in the building. We had ways of confirming the identity of those HVT who were high enough up the list of potential ISAF persons of interest to be in our sights, so we knew when they were in any particular location. Local intelligence or a long period of observation allowed us to be very sure no-one else was in the building and we then would use a Harrier dropped 500lb bomb to destroy the building and its contents. On 15th May 2009 an RAF Harrier suffered a fuel fire after messing up a perceived high threat landing and the pilot ejected on the Kandahar strip. The Harrier had been on CAP and the pilot had worked with us a few weeks previously; luckily, he was fine. We also lost a predator which had a malfunction on landing, and we took a few rounds through one of my chinooks, and suffered rear undercarriage damage during an assault onto a compound but thankfully that was all. Rocket strikes by the Taliban were quite common against our base, but only once did they land anywhere near my aircraft dispersal slightly peppering one of the chinooks with fragments whilst we took cover behind blast walls nearby.

Towards the end of my tour the UK introduced the Paveway IV dual mode GPS/INS and laser-guided bomb manufactured by Raytheon UK to the theatre. The weapon is a guidance kit based on the existing Enhanced Paveway II Enhanced Computer Control Group (ECCG) added to a modified Mk 82 general-purpose bomb with increased penetration performance. The new ECCG contains a Height of Burst (HOB) sensor enabling air burst fusing options, and a SAASM (Selective Availability Anti Spoofing Module) compliant GPS receiver. It can be launched either using inertial measurement or using GPS guidance. Terminal laser guidance is available in either navigation mode. I occasionally used this weapon against a range of targets. As the weapon was very new, I got back into the books to make sure I fully understood its possible uses and things like fragment pattern, penetration etcetera so I could match its use to specific target types.

My first operational use of Paveway IV resulted in a confirmed strike from a UK Harrier on a remote target specifically chosen to likely be miles away from any other Taliban. We wanted to be able to inspect the target post-strike in order to assess the effectiveness of the Paveway using the technique I devised. Around 45 minutes after the drop we landed alongside the target – there had been no movement since the strike, and we were certain the occupants had been killed. On inspection we found that the target was absolutely peppered with fragment holes, and there was no way the 4 occupants could have survived. The target individual had lost most of his arm and although I hardly noticed at the time, this later reminded me of the 1995 Mendig Lynx crash, and the injuries suffered by the aircraft commander as he was thrown clear of the aircraft. Much later, the image I repeatedly saw when suffering from flashbacks was the two individuals, one a friend, one an enemy both struck down with the same injuries. As usual with successful coalition strikes against HVT we carefully removed the bodies and returned with them to our base where they were respectfully buried in accordance with Muslim traditions. This was partly out of respect for our enemies but also to sow discord and doubt into the minds of the remaining Taliban as they would never know whether their comrades had died in action or decided to give up the fight and quietly disappear.

We regularly flew up to Kabul in one of the C130 to visit the Embassy and the intelligence section based in HQ ISAF. The vehicle journey from the airport to the Embassy and to HQ ISAF was through the centre of the city along one of the main thoroughfares, a dual carriageway. The dual carriageway "Airport Road" was unlike any other I've ever travelled along – crowded with bicycles, horse drawn carts, flocks of goats; concrete blocks divided the oncoming traffic but everything else was a free-for-all and the opportunity for an ambush against my vehicle (often a lone vehicle) always uppermost in my mind. To that end there were always 2 of us fully armed in the car or SUV, and it was armoured. In constant radio contact with the Embassy, they would have called out the QRF if we had been attacked and survived the bomb or RPG led attack.

Bagram Airbase lies some 50 kilometers north of Kabul. We regularly flew into Bagram in the C-130. First of all, we constantly liaised with US troops and their intelligence cells, but we also discussed tactics with other nationalities as well. One of these visits led to the Australian troops asking to "borrow" my chinooks for a particular mission. Clearance for this went right to the top as losing one or both of them would have severely impacted our operational flexibility and performance as these Chinooks would have had to be replaced by chinooks operated by the JHC out of Bastion. The Australians were without their own air support package, and this gave them the chance to go against one of the key HVTs in their

AOR.  After a day or so training and learning our techniques the mission went ahead with a UK Predator overhead in overwatch and with a direct radio link to the chinooks so I could call them off at any stage of the mission if I felt the risk was too high.  The mission was a success.

There were a few occasions where we operated beyond flying time from either of my fixed bases.  This meant deploying on our own onto a desert-based airstrip in the middle of the desert, flying in and providing all the fuel, water and food required and security for our temporary base from within our own resources.  Around 200km due South of Garmsir (itself about 150km SW of Kandahar on the Helmand River) on the border with Pakistan lies Bahram Chah, a burgeoning market set amongst a 30 or so dusty mud walled compounds and rudimentary buildings.  This was a prime location for the import of bombs and bomb making material.  We were occasionally fed information on the movements of "senior" bomb makers and facilitators or trainers.  These latter individuals were prime targets to watch – so we could see who else was involved in their bomb making chains, and then to capture or kill.  Usually, the capture missions would take place closer to the Green Zone but occasionally we would deploy to another location, set up a FOB with limited security, bring in fuel and then operate remotely from my base for a couple of days, landing Chinook in the desert with everything else being brought in by my C-130.  Fast air support would fly from Kandahar as they had the legs to remain airborne with air-to-air refueling such a long distance from base.  Any missed capture target would almost certainly head south for Bahram Chah to cross the international border at the closest point.  UK Harriers dropping bombs freefall called in by our troops hidden on the ground, confirmed by Reaper footage, accounted for a number of HVT during my tour, the issue (and final authority for the drop falling on my shoulders) being the possibility of women and children being present in the mud walled houses of the bazar. We went to extraordinary efforts watching target individuals and buildings for days on end before actioning a strike of one form or another to ensure no innocent collateral damage.

# Chapter 23.

## *N*orthern Afghanistan based ops – Flying Afghan Air Force Helicopters.

The second part of my job in Afghanistan was to oversee helicopter support to the UK mentored counter narcotics operation based out of a location in Northeastern Afghanistan. Whenever I travelled up to the North, I would make sure I spent a day or so with the aviation team there, flying out with them in the Afghan Air Force helicopters if possible, and generally making sure they were happy and being provided with whatever they needed. One day we flew the choppers out to the site of the Buddha of Bamyan overlooking the remarkably fertile stretch of the Bamyan River some 100km West of Kabul – the remains of a giant 5th-century stone Buddha carved in a cliff had been destroyed by the Taliban back in 2001 but I wanted to see the site. The near vertical cliffs with the head and shoulders shaped cut-out where the statue had stood for centuries was incredibly impressive; but it was so sad that the actual statue had been turned into dust. I had command of several choppers painted in Afghan Air Force blue based in a small camp located just outside the airfield boundary where the pilots, maintainers, ground-crew and operations staff lived. Operational sorties could originate from the "ramp" at a northern airfield or from a very remote tactical base in the mountains close to the Pakistan border around 30 kilometers from Kabul. With no roads in the area, UK PLC had built a dirt strip alongside the tactical base with just enough length to allow a C-130 to land and take off safely.

Flying the C130 out of Kabul we often had an IMC[43] climb and descent into the remote tactical location using the radar fitted to the

---

[43] IMC – Instrument meteorological Conditions – or simply "in the clouds"

aircraft and GPS to keep us from flying into the mountainside. I clearly remember one trip which was in cloud from take-off until just before landing, in itself nothing special but here we could occasionally catch a fleeting glimpse of "Cumulo-granite" or the surrounding mountain sides, just metres off our wingtip as we climbed out of Kabul, and then only see the ground we were literally seconds away from landing on once we popped out of the dense cloud cover which ended only a hundred feet or so above the mountainous dirt landing strip; exciting stuff!

Helicopters could also operate there of course, and the Russian designed Afghan choppers were well suited to this terrain. Flown originally by specially selected British AAC, RN and RAF helicopter pilots the long-term aim was to qualify Afghanistan Air Force pilots to fly the choppers themselves (through a training program based at the UK) and take over from the UK pilots, but this was well after my tour finished. The Royal Marines provided mentors to the Afghan Army counter narcotic troops who were inserted to seize or destroy opium, heroin and any other drugs found within 90 minutes flying time radius of the tactical location. Operating at night on NVG, the British pilots under my command would fly up to 30 Afghan troops close in to manufacturing or storage sites in the mountains and valleys of Northeast Afghanistan, hoping to cut down the supply of money to the Taliban bomb makes in Helmand and outlying areas of Afghanistan. During the day it was spectacular flying country. Remaining low to minimise the time we were at treat from any one or group of Taliban gunmen it was nap of the earth flying just like my Germany days, but in a larger aircraft and with the most spectacular mountain terrain all around and usually above us. Following valleys at around 80 to 100 knots flying speed, the rotor tips seemed to be kissing the ground as we followed the twists and turns of the dried-out river valleys located all over the AOR. Lifting occasionally to fly over villages we looked down on flat rooftops coloured pink or orange depending on whether pomegranate or apricots were being dried by the local village folk.  Occasionally we would take the choppers to visit outlying villages – the Afghan troops and UK mentors would question the village seniors as to any local drug production and any Taliban activity the latter being fed back to HQ ISAF.  On one of these liaison and intelligence gathering visits I bought 5 carpets – 2 for the sitting room and dining room, a gorgeous "runner" and 2 bedside carpets for my kids.  I paid well below the price I expected – probably a $20^{th}$ of their value back in the UK but the local weavers were very happy with the deal.  The carpets were shipped home at the end of my tour and remind me every day of the amazing resilience and friendliness of the average Afghan family.

# Chapter 24.

**Home Again.** Having had a period of post-tour leave I returned to Middle Wallop to my role as Chief of Staff at the AAC Centre for a few months normality until I came up for posting in the normal fashion. During these few months I found that I could get anxious about silly things, but not overbearingly so, and as time went on the panic attacks eased off and then stopped. I didn't speak to the medics at Middle Wallop nor mention the odd feelings to anyone. I didn't want it to have any lasting effect on my career.

A few months after I left Afghanistan, on December 30, 2009, al-Qaida scored perhaps its greatest success ever against the Central Intelligence Agency and its Jordanian partner service. A triple agent blew himself up at Forward Operating Base Chapman — a U.S. military base in Khost, Afghanistan some 350 km Northeast of Kandahar— killing seven CIA officers and one Jordanian officer. I visited Camp Chapman many times during my tour. The emotional impact of these deaths added to the turmoil I felt later when the PTSD reared its head full-on.

# Chapter 25.

## Head Army Digitisation Training Team – Royal Signals HQ Blandford Forum.

A few months after returning from Afghanistan I took over a role dedicated to training the Army in digitisation – an interesting and challenging role with absolutely nothing to do with flying. I had a great time working out of Blandford Camp – home to the Royal Signals, leading a team of highly qualified Warrant Officers (one for every Arm or Corps in the Army) and some very intelligent civilians designing and implementing training for the Bowman radio system, but also more interestingly for some of the right up-there electronic equipment being used by our elite infantry regiments – the Paras and the Royal Marines. The latter stuff was great – I was in and out of their barracks with new kit all the time and lots of the guys there knew me already – so there was a trust and understanding that I needed these interactions in order to maximise efforts to help these guys in theatre. For the main green, or field, Army BOWMAN was the future radio and data / planning / operational control system and producing training media which worked was great. The Army Inspectorate team came to visit. There were strict rules on how the production of training material was carried out – and I had broken almost all of them. Instead of being harangued the inspectorate team understood my points, backed up by knowledge of my recent operational experience, and decided that my methods were much better and should be utilised by other equipment training providers going forwards.

Shortly after starting at Blandford, I was called to visit HQ JHC in Wilton and whisked into Admiral Tony Johnston Burt's office (he had taken over from General Gary and was Commander JHC when I was in Afghanistan). Over a coffee we chatted about Afghanistan, and he told me that he was most disappointed that I hadn't been granted the OBE they had written me up for. Instead, and as some compensation, they had introduced a new award – A Commander JHC Commendation which had never been given to officers before. He advised that I would be getting this award and that General Gary Coward had been asked to present it to me in the near future. So not long after starting at Blandford I was asked to go to a meeting in the lecture theatre where all my men had secretly been asked to congregate, and I was presented with my citation and certificate – they now have pride of place in my downstairs loo!

# Chapter 26.

## Head of Aviation Standards – AAC Centre Middle Wallop.

Even though I enjoyed the Blandford job, I couldn't wait to get back to a flying related post, and before 2 years was up, I was very lucky to be offered a post as the Army's senior pilot, in charge of the team who set the standards all military pilots are expected to fly to, and also devise the tactics we would use to support all emerging operational or weapons led improvements. My team consisted of very highly experienced and qualified instructors ranged from Warrant Officer up to major, and between them they knew everything there was to know about flying all the army's helicopters, and also some of the RAF and RN helicopters too. Between us we flew Apache, Lynx (wheeled Mk 9 and the older Mk7 with skids), Gazelle, N3 Dauphin, Squirrel (training) and a number of others such as 212, Puma, Chinook and Sea king. There was a problem though - the field Army aviator's "view" of aviation standards was that the Aviation Standards team were long in the tooth and hadn't got any relevant and recent operational experience - which wasn't exactly their fault as they tended to be moved around posts within Standards as the "experts" for up to 6 years at a time. So, to improve our standing with the operational AAC aviation units one of the first things I did was to rotate my team of very highly experienced and qualified instructors out to Afghanistan or Iraq to spend 3 months flying with a front-line unit fighting either the Taliban or Al Qaeda. This brought their credibility with the younger aviators across the 3 services bang up to date and allowed them to check on standards across the helicopter users in a very high-pressure situation at the same time. Small corrections to techniques learnt over 3 months ago meant more safety for the crews and less risk of expensive damage and down-time for the limited number of helicopters based in theatre. At the same time, it gave a welcome extra rest period to one of the crews who had been pretty much operating on a one on 2 off regime for some years – tiring and bad for relationships at home too.

Whilst in this post I was also asked to take over the investigation into a fatal Squirrel helicopter training accident involving an AAC student and instructor where unfortunately, both were killed. Having recently qualified at Cranwell on the Air accident Investigators Course I was well placed, albeit I already had an incredibly busy job in aviation standards! After around 4 months pulling together all the evidence I was tasked to appear as the expert witness in the Coroner's Court responsible for adjudicating over the accident and in determining the cause of death of the 2 aviators, one of who I had known pretty well. The helicopter had flown into some minor power wires strung across a wooded valley, and the aircrew had not spotted them whilst flying low level on a tactical sortie towards the sun. There was a suggestion by the Court that the pilots had been erroneously wearing their dark visors when they should have lifted them and replaced them with the clear one we also had fitted to our helmets, specifically question as to why the pilots were wearing their dark visors down in a light rain shower with strong sunlight, and I was able to prove that the 2 pilots were 100% correct to be wearing their dark visors down at the time of the accident, and their deaths were logged as "accidental" and "unavoidable", which was some comfort to both families involved.

I asked for, and was granted, an extension to my tour at Aviation standards. It was incredibly satisfying work, with a fantastic team and we were thought of as being extremely useful after my changes, rather than unwanted. In fact, Commanding Officers of all the aviation regiments were clamouring for us to visit them and check them over, knowing that the command chain in HQ JHC really listened to our views and advice.

Towards the end of my tour heading up Aviation Standards I was asked to run an investigation into the crash of an RAF Chinook which happened whilst the RAF were training crews in the USA deserts for an upcoming Afghanistan deployment. The aircraft had been crewed by 2 qualified but inexperienced pilots who wrote off the aircraft whilst attempting a difficult landing technique in the desert. I was able to prove that due to their inexperience they had been flying outside the operational envelope of the chinook but that the oversight of their trip had been significantly flawed. To give the JHC command structure due credit they took onboard everything I had said was wrong in the structure of training for deployments and authorising such flights together with acceptance of unknown risks by the chain of command; and they made massive changes, which made flying safer for inexperience aircrew.

One of the more exciting, or perhaps scary, trips during my time heading up aviation standards was to sit in the back seat of a Mk 7 Lynx whilst the 2 pilots chosen to fly the display routine many will remember watching at airshows and aviation events, was flown and then signed off as being safe – by me! You might remember seeing the Lynx flipping backwards over its own tail from what looked like a very low height during the display. When tightly strapped in to the 3-man jump seat in the back, looking out between the shoulders of the 2 hands-on pilots it felt way too low, especially with no access to the controls – something most pilots hate; but it was an amazingly powerful helicopter and was a remarkably safe manoeuvre when flown by well-trained display pilots. Not one for your average front line pilot though!

# Chapter 27.

## Republique Centrafrican (Central African Republic) Head Current Ops.

After 5 fabulous years I rotated out of aviation standards and was posted to an operational tour with the EU, as Operations lead for an EU Force working to restore order to the Central African Republic (CAR) – one of the poorest and most violent countries in Africa at the time. Sadly, it still is. Law and order had been lost by the previous UN force, who had been withdrawn in a hurry, with the EU putting forward a mixed nation force to fill the gap until the UN could get their act in order. It was brutal. Shootings and mutilation of civilians as a method of subjugation, usually by machete, was rife. My job involved overseeing operations on the ground in CAR; liaising with the multi-national infantry battlegroup, French helicopter force and Foreign Legion troops together with Spanish elite forces working in-country, sorting out problems for them and passing on directions from the General in charge who was mostly based in the EU Force HQ, in Greece, just like me. I was particularly picked for this lone British post due to my past experience working with elite forces and helicopters. Here, based in seemingly innocuous central Greece, working out of a dusty Greek Army barracks in Larissa, I worked long hours and lived alone in a cheap hotel room, the only Brit amongst 120 Officers of various European Union army, air force and navy units supported by a few soldiers in administrative roles. Every other Nation sent teams of their military personnel to work in the HQ in Larissa, or on the ground in CAR, only the UK sent a sole individual; the national elements (as they were called) living usually in multi-bedroom flats, but even the smaller contingents sharing accommodation in apartments or multiple rooms in hotels. It was here, a lone Englishmen amongst many friendly EU nationals that the panic attacks became much stronger, debilitating with the ferocity of the feeling of impending doom, the building pressure inside my head, inability to breathe properly, and the blinding headaches which hit me time and time again. I also experienced occasional waking up from deep sleep unable to breathe, thinking someone was in my room and something violent was about to happen, gasping for air and unable to tell reality from the remaining dregs of the dark dream, until I could calm myself down, my brain eventually recognizing what was real and more importantly what wasn't.  The nightmare having become exceedingly real because my memory banks remembered similar real events from my past but couldn't initially tell that they were just memories!  Again, I'd try to get into fresh air whenever this happened as for some weird reason this helped settle me more quickly.  I remember very clearly standing in for my Brigadier to brief the General one morning – something I had done with ease all through my career – I couldn't catch my breath at all – I felt as if I'd run up Everest, not jogged up 3 flights of stairs, I really felt I was about to pass-out and struggled to deliver the briefing.  Once again, the overwhelming desire during the attacks was to get outside where I didn't feel so hemmed in.  One of the Belgian medics deployed to the HQ realised something was amiss and, following me out of the briefing, she persuaded me to go and see the local Greek Army doctor, who put me through a heap of tests in the local hospital, and then told me I was depressed, and prescribed some heavy drugs. Shit, I've never been depressed in my life – always up-beat and ready for anything, so what the hell was going on? After a frantic phone discussion with UK doctors at Middle Wallop – my home base, where we agreed I should take some medication, but a less strong dose of a milder "happy pill" I then went back to the Belgian doctor who discussed this with the Greek doctor, and thankfully reached agreement that I wasn't depressed, I was suffering from PTSD, and that in Greek the name for both was the same.

# Chapter 28.

## S01 Lessons Learnt – Land Warfare Centre - My last Army posting, and my mental breakdown. My symptoms of PTSD had built up slowly, through the panic attacks in Afghanistan, falling away to nothing by the time I had been back home for a few years. They then started up with a vengeance whilst deployed with EUFOR RCA with headaches, panic attacks and a feeling of dread creeping over me occasionally, especially towards the end of the tour. I really think that the 6 months spent living alone with little social exposure except for the 11 to 12 hour working days contributed enormously to the return and escalation of my symptoms. The Belgian doctor and subsequently Greek medical staff were superb, and probably prevented me descending further into the depths during my tour. Good results and a feeling of being wanted and trusted in my judgement helped in this.

Having returned from Greece / Africa feeling decidedly under the weather I was posted to Warminster to be a part of the team collating and publishing lessons learnt from wherever the Army was deployed. Within a week of starting the job I was experiencing blinding headaches and anxiety attacks daily. Things were not good. I continually woke up now fighting to breathe, shouting in my dreams and night terrors became the norm and most usually about some horrendous event happening to my children. In one particular recurring night terror my daughter slipped down an open manhole in the street after heavy rain and I was only just clinging on to her when I awoke – how strange is that? I started needing to prop myself up in bed and even put blocks under the feet at the head of my bed too. This was so that I could get out of bed quickly and run if I needed to – run from what I don't know to this day! I found that playing music quietly through earphones distracted me enough to allow me to fall asleep – with the downside that if my ipod ran out of battery power and I woke up, I had to wait for it to re-charge before I could try get to sleep again.

At work in Warminster the team were made up of alpha males who most, like me, had significant operational experience and this was a major issue for me – to look weak in front of my peers was something I just didn't want to do. With a lot of pressure to do well, the darker side of PTSD soon grew again, starting with feelings of unease and building slowly to panic attacks with violent headaches, and an overwhelming sense of anxiety becoming a daily disturbance to my work and life at home.

The most prevalent way PTSD forced its way into my life was that it reduced simple common place experiences to something where I was on the verge of panic. Hyper vigilance became a constant companion. I couldn't enter a shop or pub/restaurant without immediately working out where the exits were and forcing myself to sit where I could monitor the most obvious exit continually; this because in the back of my mind I had the never-ending loop-play tape telling me something bad was about to happen! Even going for a walk with my lovely Rhodesian Ridgeback – he who apparently sensed the exact moment I landed at RAF Brize Norton on my return to the UK after my Afghanistan tour, became a challenge. When the effects got to the stage of actually making me scared of walking through woods if there was a breeze in case the trees all fell down and crushed me, my family or my dog I knew I had a problem. When I was suffering a panic attack my brain was making it worse by taking the scenario in front of me (normally quite innocuous) but filling in any gaps with nasty memories that I hadn't had time or ability to deal with from all the horrendous accidents I'd witnessed in the past. This unaccountable anxiety grew and grew until it pervaded every experience that I normally would have loved doing. Simple DIY tasks (I built a big extension on my house almost single handed in 2011) became frightening in case it went wrong, even when it was something I'd done thousands of times in the past perfectly well. I became unable to stand having an argument and had to go for a long walk whenever my companions disagreed with me – even the slightest issues. During all of this, which was before I sought help, my overarching thoughts were worrying about what my peers would think of me if they knew how debilitating my day-to-day life had become.

I love walking in the mountains including scrambling. I took a few days off to go to Wales and climb (or walk and scramble) up Snowden and Tryfan. I had an anxiety attack on both and had to stop after scrambling only a few metres up Tryfan's rocky ladder, sliding back down to then walk around the base of Tryfan and use the Pig Track to ascend Snowden instead of the more usual Crib Gogh scramble route I had done 6 times previously.

When I started suffering flashbacks to the results of 2 most similar incidents, the Germany Mendig lynx crash and the attack on an insurgent by Paveway IV in Afghanistan, weirdly most often whilst taking a shower, I found it hard to recover and get the images out of my head, and my anxiety affected sleep patterns morphed into an inability to either get to or stay asleep I knew I had to go to the doctor for help. After managing the attacks for 3 weeks I told my new boss at Warminster, who was immediately helpful and got me to see my doctor back at Middle Wallop. Then I opened up and explained everything that had been happening to me. Initially my own doctor at Middle Wallop proscribed me some mild anti-depressants. However, I found these altered my sense of reality and I only stayed on them long enough to get my sleep patterns back into a normal rhythm. She managed to fast track me into the medical care system at Tidworth and I was booked to see the Army's top psychologist within 2 weeks. In the meantime, I had scans (MRI and CAT) to check there wasn't anything else causing the constant blinding headaches. Luckily the scans came back showing my head and body as physically very healthy. I saw the top Army clinical psychologist in Tidworth, and he quickly and unequivocally diagnosed me as suffering from PTSD, just as the Greek Army doctor had done. He was at lengths to explain that the majority of people he saw had never or rarely seen violent death, especially of people they knew, had almost never been responsible for the death of others, and that most who were diagnosed with PTSD were either elite Forces members or senior pilots in the 3 services who had seen a lot of accidents or action. I fitted both! He rarely saw infantrymen or other soldiers as the key problem was in his view, seeing death close up usually on multiple occasions spread over a long time - often very violent death and often of close friends, who one was unable to help. Contrary to expectation infantrymen don't see as much death as some pilots; they often see horrendous things (and in Afghanistan unfortunately this was very true during the latter part of the first 10 years of the post Twin Towers era) with friends being maimed and killed by IEDs, but it is usually over a concentrated period of months and for some reason this doesn't have as much effect on the human brain as long term exposure. It is absolutely awful, but the long-term mental effects are often not as great as the physical short-term ones.

Surprisingly perhaps, the Army was brilliant. Not one alpha male ever said anything detrimental to me about suffering from PTSD, and in fact those closest to me as friends, and as work colleagues all bent over backwards to make me feel comfortable. Initially, straight after my diagnosis, I was told to take a few weeks off which I did. I slept straight through for hours and hours at a time. Whenever I woke up with an anxiety attack or another horrendous nightmare, I would plug in my ipod and listen to my favourite music quietly in the background. Sometimes I was too anxious to get to sleep and sat up in bed listening to music into the small hours before I eventually fell into a fitful sleep. After the 3-week break my boss told me to come in whenever I felt things were okay, and to go home whenever I felt ill without having to ask permission. I built up my working periods from mornings only to around 6 hours a day over a period of around a month. I was responsible for speaking to returning troops and seeing if there were any emerging lessons which would benefit troops in training or about to deploy to Afghanistan and Iraq. Weirdly, I really enjoyed the work and was able to use other people's experiences to mitigate my more disturbing ones.

During the last 6 months of my military service, I received counselling weekly, going through a whole series of exploratory thinking to identify the real triggers of my PTSD, then identifying what caused those triggers to tip me over the edge. The Individual Cognitive Behavioural Therapy was just what I needed to be able to process why I was suffering. The counsellors and I together worked out that there were 2 elements to my PTSD: guilt based on seeing friends killed and not being able to do anything for them, and the Taliban deaths which I felt responsible for even though I hadn't actually physically pulled any trigger during my tour in Afghanistan. We also worked out that the spark-point for the PTSD was seeing the Taliban soldier who had lost his arm in the Paveway strike which reminded me so much of the 1994 Mendig lynx accident aircraft commander who had been thrown clear of the disintegrating Lynx and had lost an arm in the process. This was the starting point for the long struggle to get better.

As time went on, using the ICBT (with help from 2 amazing staff sergeant counsellors) I was able to work out how to counter the negative thoughts and get myself through any attacks with the minimum impact on my performance and my daily life. I still had the flashbacks, but I wasn't frightened by them, and exploring them in detail made me realise that there was absolutely nothing I could have done in any early accidents to save the girl killed in the glider, the 2 pilots burned to death in the Lynx near Soest, or the aircraft commander and pilot killed at Mendig. I began to understand that I wasn't a bad person for being responsible for neutralising several HVT, which had undoubtably led to saving the lives of numerous servicemen and women on the ground in Afghanistan. Although it sounds obvious now, my concerns over this had somehow got entwined with my guilt over the accidents where I couldn't help friends and colleagues. It took some dragging out of me and realisation & reinforcement by the councillors to allow me to change my perception and form the view that dealing with the Taliban HVT led to a significant reduction in risk for coalition troops, and that led to a significant fall in coalition deaths and those of Afghan nationals caught up in insurgent attacks; and that what I had done in Afghanistan and Africa, whilst lethal for those involved, had been a good thing in the wider sense.

Funnily enough, I only really began to get over the PTSD when able to talk more freely about it, choked up during my talks to the members and visitors at Lasham, and in receipt of a handful of amazing letters from listeners who thanked me for my service and for what I had done through my career but particularly in Afghanistan and CAR. High performing people with good jobs who had no idea what soldiers can go through whilst giving up their time, and sadly sometimes their lives, in service to the country in peacetime and in war.


I still occasionally get anxious over silly things, but can usually see it in myself, and can talk myself out of it mostly. My gorgeous girlfriend sees it starting when it occasionally does surface and lets me know, never judging, just helping. I thank her for giving me the courage to write this story, it undoubtably assists the healing process to talk to people and writing my story down has proven amazingly cathartic.

*Figure 26 - My "rack" after 31 years' Service & 7 Operational Tours*

# Chapter 29.

**Return to Civilian Life.** I decided that I should leave the Army a little earlier than originally planned – I couldn't risk the PTSD flaring up again if deployed and I couldn't in all moral honesty consider myself as "serving" if I was undeployable. Not when young men and women were still being killed in action in Afghanistan and in Iraq. I had a brilliant 31 years in the Army, serving with the most fantastic young men and women, and also being lucky enough to not only fly helicopters throughout my career, but also work on operations directly in support of Britain's elite troops. I was tied into giving 7 months' notice at the time – standard for a long serving officer, but when I landed my current job in my first job interview in 32 years my military boss persuaded Glasgow HR branch that I should be allowed to leave within the 3 months the new employers needed. I spent the last 3 months of my career pulling together the final chapters of the Operation HERRICK Lessons Learnt Report – a fascinating task where I met some amazing individuals who had also had really interesting careers, to talk through their experiences and draw out lessons for others soon to follow.

In 2016 I left the army after 31 years. I went back to my roots and took a position managing the biggest gliding club in the World.

# Chapter 30.

## Coming to Terms with PTSD long term.

Unlike some others, I enjoyed moving on from the Army, new challenges and new people lay ahead. The one thing I did miss was the camaraderie and the willingness of serving personnel to get stuck in, and to get the job done whatever the challenges. Having spent a year running the gliding club – a significant enterprise managing an estate of around 500 acres, looking after the clubs' buildings and 800 members with 200+ gliders on site, managing the output of 23 permanent staff and overseeing a turnover of around £1.3m annually, I did find myself becoming anxious if things were not going as smoothly as I would have expected, but I didn't descend back into the outright horror of PTSD.

The techniques I had learnt during my rehabilitation worked well, I could recognise the signs of an approaching panic attack and prevent it occurring. I was rather surprised to be asked to talk about my career at one of the club's "winter talks". These bi-weekly talks took place during winter evenings when the normally frenetic gliding activity has to be curtailed due to short days and sometimes poor weather. I wasn't sure anyone would want to listen to me droning on about my experiences gliding as a youngster and then later flying helicopters in the Army, but I found the process cathartic especially the last few minutes where I would tell them a little of how I had felt when suffering from PTSD at its worst, choking back tears and struggling to speak for a few minutes.

I was amazed to be asked to "do it again" the following year, and again the next – around 280 gliding club members listened to my talks over the 3 years and donated a considerable sum towards my chosen charity – "Combat Stress".

What I found amazing was that talking about my suffering with

PTSD became less difficult each time and a significant number of the visitors to my talks wrote me a personal letter afterwards, some expressing their appreciation of my service, some of a "job well done" and others admiring how I had managed to come through a seriously debilitating bout of PTSD and come to terms with it, and what I had seen and done throughout and before my military career.

I found that, in line with the emerging ways of youth in this great country, including HRH Princes William and Harry, that talking about mental health problems in a constructive way was beneficial in 2 ways: it lessened the impact personally and it opened the way for others suffering similarly to ask for help. It is now widely known that PTSD can affect anybody at any time if exposed to a traumatic stimulus. Some people affected are able to get over their experience and recover more easily than others. Some, very sadly, commit suicide at a later date when stuck in the midst of the seemingly perfect storm of intense internal pressure and unfortunate lack of resources available to help them get past the worst, unable to learn how to cope with their individual demons. I was incredibly lucky, I got top performing specialists advising and assisting me through the period following diagnosis of my troubles.

I wrote this book initially to help myself, but in hindsight I hope it has increased awareness of PTSD and how it can affect and debilitate even some of the most stable and confident individuals. If this book has raised an interest in PTSD in you please give money to "Combat Stress" or one of the other organisations which help all sorts of people through a horrendous mental experience – it is not just the military and civil services (police, fire and NHS front line staff) who can suffer, it is anyone who experiences anything from a single traumatic event through constant milder exposure which eventually reaches that individual's tipping point.

# *E*nd point:

Thank you for buying this book. Some of the proceeds will be given to charity specialising in helping retired servicemen and women with PTSD.

I amassed approximately 2,200 hours in command of military rotary wing, or helicopters, during my varied and often exciting career.

I still suffer from the lasting effects of PTSD, but I have learnt to cope with them. Occasional anxiety when not really warranted is the lasting effect, but I am alive, I had fun, and I served my Country. What more could a person want? The best bit is the camaraderie and instant understanding that exists between anyone who has deployed on an operational tour where lives are at risk. It is a bond most who have not done it will never understand, but I hope this book will help them to do that, and possibly make the British Armed Forces seem a little less distant from their daily lives. You are surrounded by men and women who have served their country, some for just 3 years, some for more than I. They are the salts of this earth, know what it is to give to others without condition, and to risk absolutely everything for the common good. They will usually say nothing about their experiences of keeping the population at large safer than they would be without a professional Armed Forces, but just might if you ask. If you have enjoyed reading this book, and even better it has helped you to understand the military experience, please give a little more to my chosen military mental health charity by donating at my "just giving" page which can be found at the following URL: justgiving.com/page/gav-spink-1700746002251.

My career as an aviator in the British Army spanned 31 years with the more interesting elements listed below:

1985: Royal Military Academy Sandhurst – 7 January - December 1985.

1986: Army Pilots Course (APC 294) at Middle Wallop: May 1986 to December 1986.

1987 – 1988: 3 Regt AAC Soest, Germany (BAOR)

1988: 8-month Operational Tour – Northern Ireland, 665 Sqn NI Regiment AAC

1989-1990: Adjutant 9 Regt AAC – Liaison Flying UK

1990-92: Chief Signals Instructor – Depot Regt AAC – Middle Wallop AAC Centre – Liaison Flying UK

1991: 6-month Operational Tour - Gulf War One/UNIKOM Kuwait and Iraq

1993: Studying for MSc Degree in Guided Weapon Systems

1994-1996: Command of 661 Sqn, 1 Regt AAC, Gutersloh, Germany

1995-6: 9-month Operational Tour Bosnia: 661 Sqn AAC - UNPROFOR & IFOR.

1997-1998: MoD PE – Air Armaments (Apache weapons)

1998-2001: Second in Command – 1 Regt AAC, Gutersloh, Germany

2001-2003: Command of 29 Flt AAC – BATUS, Alberta, Canada

2003-2006: Staff appointment as Lt Col HQ Land Wilton (no flying)

2006 – 2009: Staff appointment as COS Army Aviation Centre, Middle Wallop (some liaison flying)

2008/9: 6-month Op Tour - Command of specialist aviation unit in Afghanistan

2009 - 2011: Head of the Digitised Training Development Team based in Blandford

**224**

2011-2015: Head of Army Aviation Standards, AAC Centre, Middle Wallop

2015: 5-month Op Tour – Lead G3 Ops – EUFOR-RCA Greece & Central African Republic

April 2015 to April 2016: SO1 Lead Lessons Collection – Land Warfare School, Warminster.

Printed in Great Britain
by Amazon